PRATCHETT

The Adventures of
Paddington   MICHAEL BOND

THE CO...

D0716253

Windsor and Maidenhead

95800000159739

Kate Young is an award-winning food writer, cook and bookworm. Her first book, *The Little Library Cookbook*, was shortlisted for the Fortnum & Mason Debut Food Book Award, and won a World Gourmand food writing award. Her second, *The Little Library Year*, a literary and culinary almanac, was shortlisted for the General Cookbook Award by the Guild of Food Writers. She was named Blogger of the Year in 2017 by the Guild of Food Writers. To read more of her work, visit her blog (thelittlelibrarycafe.com), or follow her (@bakingfiction) on Twitter and Instagram. She is based in the English countryside.

Lean Timms is a freelance travel, food and lifestyle photographer. Although born in Australia, Lean has been lucky enough to photograph for editorials and publications throughout the world. She is based in Canberra, Australia.

THE
LITTLE
LIBRARY
CHRISTMAS

KATE
YOUNG

HEAD
of ZEUS

an Anima Book

For my family (all my families).
In memory of Christmases past,
anticipation of this Christmas present,
and for the promise of Christmases
yet to come.

CONTENTS

Presently she came to the market square where the Christmas market was going on. There were stalls of turkeys and geese, fruit stalls with oranges, apples, nuts, and tangerines that are like small oranges wrapped in silver paper. Some stalls had holly, mistletoe, and Christmas trees, some had flowers; there were stalls of china and glass and one with wooden spoons and bowls. A woman was selling balloons and an old man was cooking hot chestnuts.

The Story of Holly and Ivy, Rumer Godden

If you have read my previous books, then it will come as no great surprise to hear that I adore Christmas. There are pages and recipes and reminiscences dedicated to it in both *The Little Library Cookbook* and *The Little Library Year*, and you now sit with this third, entirely Christmas-focused one, in your hands. But, unless you have spent Christmas in my company, you may not be aware of the sheer degree to which I look forward to it every year. The anticipation and planning consumes a good eight weeks of my calendar – from early November, when I make my holiday playlist, book my cinema tickets, pull my favourite Christmas books down from the shelf, and start to consider parties and menus. It ramps up once Advent arrives, when I start cooking in earnest, filling jars with jams and preserves to give as gifts, putting my tree up, inviting friends round to celebrate, and making my Christmas puddings. It continues into Christmas week, and through that in-between period in the run up to New Year's Eve, then all the way into January, only ending when I arrange for my Christmas tree to be collected on Epiphany.

I approach the season with boundless enthusiasm and a desire for everything to be as Christmassy as possible. And so, over my three decades of celebrating it, I have eaten a lot of Christmas food, watched an obscene number of Christmas films, read all the Christmas books I can lay my hands on, and listened to approximately 63 versions of *O Holy Night* (from the King's College Cambridge choir to *NSYNC). In short, when it comes to Christmas, I am all in.

I'm not for a minute suggesting that you need to do the same – perhaps you don't really engage with the holiday until the middle of December arrives, or maybe your celebrations are restricted to the day itself. But I am assuming, if you have this book in your kitchen, that you're a fan of Christmas too. That you get excited by the prospect of a goose (or a glossy ham, or a vegetarian wellington) on the table, by a batch of mince pies coming out of the oven, by a jug of eggnog that has just been mixed up. That you enjoy stringing twinkling lights around your windows, and decorating the tree, and that you're inclined to hover by the brass bands and a cappella singing groups that take up residence in railway stations during December.

Long before I moved to the UK, and began to shape my Christmases into what they now are, I had a sense of what the season here would be like. So much of my early obsession with England was borne of the contents of my bookshelves, and so Christmas in the cold felt oddly familiar. From my bedroom in Australia, I spent Christmas with Shirley Hughes' Lucy and Tom, with Noel Streatfeild's various families, with C. S. Lewis' Pevensie children and the Beavers, and with Tove Jansson's Moomins. I followed them through snow, and into their cosy homes, filled with the familiar scents of cinnamon, nutmeg, and a bird roasting in the oven.

Thanks to well-trodden rituals, to the universality of so many traditions, Christmas is, narratively speaking, a useful time to set a story. There's a shorthand to it – a kind of magic that can only happen when characters are no longer consumed by the regular day to day. It's a way of bringing people together in a place where the inevitable romantic declarations, family drama, and revelations can take place around a crowded dinner table dressed with holly and lit by candles. It's easy to explain characters saying slightly more than they mean to when they're drunk on eggnog, or feeling claustrophobic after days spent in close proximity. And so Christmas scenes often pop up in books that aren't ostensibly 'about' Christmas: Emma rejects Mr Elton (after he rejects the very idea of Miss Smith) after a Christmas party, Jane Eyre makes preparations for Christmas when she stays with her cousins, Bathsheba Everdene hosts a Christmas party in *Far from the Madding Crowd*, Nikolai and Sonya prepare a pantomime in *War and Peace*.

It is woven too into *Bridget Jones's Diary*, *The Secret Diary of Adrian Mole Aged 13¾*, *The Diary of a Nobody* and *The Diary of a Provincial Lady* – it could hardly be absent from books which take us through a year in the life of their characters. We expect, as we approach December, that the thoughts of our narrator will turn to gift giving, to parties, to turkey, because it is unavoidable in our own lives. It is, in these stories, an inevitability; a diary would be strange and incomplete without it.

Many of the books in the pages to come were, unsurprisingly, written with children in mind. Like so many Christmas traditions – hanging stockings, dressing the tree, making gingerbread houses – there is an unmistakably childlike joy intrinsic in their celebration. Though I don't buy into the rhetoric that Christmas is for children (I like it far too much to leave it to them entirely), I understand why images from Christmases in children's literature are so iconic: the

Pevensie siblings meeting Santa Claus in Narnia, the Great Hall at Hogwarts decked for the occasion, the Grinch sneaking off with a sack of stolen presents, a meal of hot chocolate and Turkish delight aboard the Polar Express. There is something truly magical about Christmas that invites us to shelve our cynicism, to lean into the joy, to find reasons to celebrate.

And so here, in the pages that follow, is a collection of reasons to celebrate. There are edible gifts to make, musings on Christmas trees, recipes for parties, and thoughts about quiet nights in. There are menus and plans for Christmas Eve, Christmas Day and New Year's Day, suggestions for leftovers, a longing for snow, and memories of gingerbread houses. This Christmas, and in Christmases to come, I want this book to be a friend to you in your planning, and your cooking, offering suggestions, inspiration and advice. And so I very much hope that the reminiscences, recipes, and beloved books you find here bring a little seasonal joy into your home – and, most specifically, into your kitchen.

Our hearts grow tender with childhood memories and love of kindred, and we are better throughout the year for having, in spirit, become a child again at Christmastime.

Laura Ingalls Wilder

Notes on Recipes

My recipes have been tried and tested in my conventional (non-fan) oven. If you have a fan oven, simply reduce cooking temperatures by 20°C.

All recipes use whole milk, salted butter, and large eggs, unless otherwise specified.

ESSENTIAL KITCHEN EQUIPMENT

Baking dishes, sheets and pans
Chopping knife and board
Fork, knife and spoon
Frying pan/skillet
Paper towels
Parchment paper and greaseproof/
  wax paper
Plastic wrap and foil
Large and small saucepans
Measuring jug/cup

Mixing bowls
Sieve/strainer
Spatula
Sterilized jars for preserves
Tea towel/dish towel
Thermometer
Vegetable peeler
Whisk
Wire/cooling rack
Wooden spoon

BROWN
PAPER
PACKAGES

It was not like the Christmases at St Leonard's-on-Sea when, for days beforehand, the bell never stopped ringing as gifts of all kinds were delivered – but especially useful, helpful presents from the parishioners. In those days the tradespeople with whom you dealt sent presents: a turkey from the butcher; a box of crystallized fruits or chocolates from the grocer; fruit from the greengrocer.

A Vicarage Family, Noel Streatfeild

I love giving presents. I look forward to hours spent in bookstores, browsing the shelves and considering which novel I've read and loved that a particular friend might enjoy. I relish the chance to make plans for a dinner or find tickets to something perfect. I love time spent at the stove, filling jars with something I hope the recipient will find delicious. Despite this, there's always a night, sometime in early December, when I wake with a start, thanks to the gnawing realization that I have yet to decide on or purchase a single Christmas gift. It's not a feeling I am comfortable with; I am, generally, quite an organized person. I love a list, and an Excel spreadsheet. I spent the early part of my professional life as a theatre producer, so planning is not unfamiliar to me. But despite the Christmas season always arriving with inescapable fanfare, I let that fear creep in every year.

The problem is, shopping for Christmas gifts doesn't feel 'right' to me any earlier than December. I know plenty of people get started early every year – their presents squirreled away in drawers and cupboards, to be brought out when needed. But I don't want to be thinking about Christmas in August, when the days are long and hot. I want to enjoy the process of gathering gifts, as part of the season.

Like most other people I know, I now do the lion's share of my shopping online. My groceries are brought to my door during a distinct window of time, the internet is the best and most reliable place to lay my hands on hard-to-find ingredients (especially now that I don't live in London), and I'm not left navigating a journey home with slightly too much shopping over my shoulders. But at Christmas, all that changes. The high street is lit up with strings of fairy lights, and brass bands playing carols pop up on street corners. In my town, the weekly Saturday market fills with wreaths, handmade gifts, the best varieties of apples, and cuts of Gloucestershire pork. It's crowded, and overwhelming, and slightly stressful, and I absolutely love it.

Like those sending gifts to the family in *The Vicarage Family*, my budget has never stretched to being able to send a hamper from Fortnum & Mason, and so batch-making edible gifts has become a yearly tradition. The first year I did it out of necessity. I was short on cash due to a financial Bermuda Triangle: new job with an elusive first pay cheque, a hefty deposit on the flat, and an unfurnished room that needed a bed, and so I decided to turn the cheap bowls of ingredients I found on Ridley Road Market into jars of chutneys and bottles of cordials and boxes of homemade biscuits. It was joyous – the cooking relaxed me during a stressful time, and the sight of my efforts, encased in mismatched glass jars in my kitchen, was a tangible reminder of celebrations and good meals on the horizon. It's now something I eagerly anticipate – even if I do always leave it slightly too late. Ending up in my kitchen at 2 a.m., four days before Christmas, covered in icing sugar and sticky with chutney is, after all, a little tradition in its own right.

Potted Stilton with rosemary and rye crackers

Long after the sun has set on Christmas Day, once lunch has settled, though with hours still before bed, everyone in our house starts glancing around sheepishly, flummoxed to find themselves in pursuit of something to nibble on. A cheeseboard is always the answer. This potted Stilton is simple, but undeniably impressive: perfect for gifting. It always makes me think of Louise and her cousins in Elizabeth Jane Howard's *Marking Time*, for whom Stilton is a rare Christmas luxury. This is an ideal way to eke it out.

MAKES A 350ML/12OZ POT OF CHEESE AND 20 CRACKERS

POTTED STILTON
200g/7oz Stilton, rind removed
140g/5oz butter, softened
1tbsp Port or sherry
10 green peppercorns in brine

RYE AND ROSEMARY CRACKERS
35g/¼ cup plain/all-purpose flour, plus extra if needed

40g/generous ¼ cup dark rye flour
A pinch of fine salt
1tsp caster/superfine sugar
3 sprigs rosemary, leaves finely chopped
40ml/2½tbsp water
1tbsp olive oil
A pinch of flaky salt

1. To prepare the potted Stilton, crumble the cheese into a bowl, and then mash half of the softened butter through it.

2. Add the port or sherry, and mix it through. Spoon the mixture into a bowl or ramekin, and level off the top.

3. Melt the rest of the butter with the peppercorns. Leave to cool a little, then pour over the top of the cheese. Cover with a sheet of greaseproof/wax paper, and place in the fridge for a good couple of hours (or a few days, if that's easier) before gifting it. The cheese will keep like this for a month.

4. For the crackers, preheat the oven to 200°C/400°F/Gas 6. Put the flours, fine salt, sugar, and half the chopped rosemary into a bowl. Mix the water with the oil, and pour over the dry ingredients, bringing the dough together with your hands. If it is unmanageably sticky, add a little more plain flour.

5. Lay a sheet of greaseproof/wax paper on your work surface. On top of this paper (or they'll be tricky to lift up and move about later), roll the dough out as thinly as you can – the thinner they are, the crisper they will be.

6. Cut into squares, or circles, and reshape the offcuts. Brush the crackers with a little water, prick each one a couple of times with a fork and then sprinkle the rest of the rosemary and the flaky salt over the top.

7. Place the crackers on a lined baking sheet, with a little space between each one, and bake for 12–15 minutes until golden and crisp. Cool on a wire/cooling rack and then store in an airtight container for up to a week.

Apple, pear and chilli chutney

I've borrowed the method for this chutney from Theresa's date and apple one in Diana Henry's *Salt, Sugar, Smoke*. The preparation – a good twenty minutes of chopping everything into a small dice, unless you're a savant with a knife – takes a little time, but I assure you the results are worth it. I make big saucepans full of this, year after year, and end up keeping as much as I give away. It has proved a worthy partner to every cheese I have tested it with so far.

MAKES 4 X 300ML/10OZ JARS

1kg/2¼lb eating apples, peeled, cored and finely diced
500g/1lb 2oz pears, peeled, cored and finely diced
500g/1lb 2oz onions, peeled and finely diced

500g/2½ cups granulated sugar
300ml/1¼ cups cider vinegar
1tsp fine salt
1tsp chilli flakes

1. Place the fruit and onions in a large saucepan, and cook over a low heat for an hour, stirring regularly so they don't stick. The apples will give off plenty of liquid, so you don't need to add any at this stage.

2. After an hour, stir in the sugar, vinegar, salt, and chilli. Bring to a simmer and reduce until thickened, stirring regularly. To check if it is done, draw a line along the bottom of the pan with the spoon; when the chutney is ready, the line won't flood with liquid.

3. Spoon into sterilized jars. The chutney will keep in a cool, dark place for at least 6 months, but has yet to last that long at my place.

Pickled sprouts

There is, of course, a sprouts recipe for Christmas Day on p127, but as this is a book about Christmas, I decided I could get away with including two. Though they have a chequered reputation, I adore Brussels sprouts. I long for an annual sprout festival like the one alluded to (albeit infuriatingly briefly) in Terry Pratchett's *Hogfather*. In lieu of this, I have dedicated myself to finding a way to include them in as many meals as possible. Pickling leaves them tender and full of flavour, perfect for serving alongside bubble and squeak, with soft cheeses on a cheeseboard, or on their own, straight from the jar.

MAKES ENOUGH TO FILL A 1-LITRE/34OZ JAR

750g/1lb 10oz Brussels sprouts
500ml/2 cups distilled malt vinegar
10g/2tsp fine salt
50g/¼ cup granulated sugar
½tsp chilli flakes

1tbsp coriander seeds
3 star anise
1tbsp fennel seeds
2 bay leaves
1tsp black peppercorns

1. Clean the sprouts, and remove any yellowed or browning outer leaves. Slice them in half (don't trim the stem unless they are long and woody, or they will fall apart). Put the sprouts in a colander.

2. Bring a pan half filled with water to the boil. Place the colander on top, and cover with a lid. The water shouldn't touch the sprouts – you want them to steam, not boil – so tip a little out if needs be. Don't worry about the lid fitting perfectly; you just want to keep a bit of the steam in. Steam for 3 minutes, then remove from the heat.

3. Put the vinegar, salt, sugar and spices in a saucepan, and bring to a simmer. Once the salt and sugar have dissolved, turn the heat off.

4. Push the sprouts into a sterilized jar and pour the pickling liquid on top. Leave for at least two weeks before opening the jar.

A box of roasted nuts

These are delicious at any time of year, but there's something particularly jolly about a box of them at Christmas – especially with this spicing. They would be fantastic served as the nuts are on Christmas night in *The Mill on the Floss*: on a board alongside some glorious oranges, apple jelly, and damson cheese.

MAKES 400G/3 CUPS

400g/3 cups mixed nuts (anything you fancy, really, though I tend to include almonds, cashews, walnuts and Brazil nuts)
2tbsp honey
2tbsp groundnut or vegetable oil

1tsp ground cinnamon
½tsp ground nutmeg
½tsp smoked paprika
A pinch of ground black pepper
1tsp flaky salt, plus extra if needed
1tbsp chopped rosemary

1. Preheat the oven to 170°C/325°F/Gas 3. Lay the nuts in a single layer on a baking sheet and roast for 15 minutes.

2. Place the remaining ingredients in a small saucepan, and melt together over a low heat.

3. Pour the spiced honey over the nuts, toss well to coat, and return to the oven for another 10 minutes. Taste, and season with some additional salt if needed. Serve warm, or tip into a jar once completely cool to keep for up to a week.

Cranberry cordial

I first made this to use in place of peach purée in a wintry Bellini and I loved it so much that now I always have a bottle of it in the fridge over Christmas. It's a vibrant, festive red, and is delicious served topped up with soda or tonic water, with fizzy wine (one part cordial to three parts fizz), or in a 50:50 mix with vodka or gin, ideally shaken with some ice.

MAKES ABOUT 1 LITRE/4¼ CUPS

1kg/2¼lb fresh or frozen cranberries
1 litre/4¼ cups water
500g/2 cups caster/superfine sugar
3 cinnamon sticks

Strips of zest and juice from 5 lemons

EQUIPMENT
A piece of muslin/cheesecloth

1. Pour the cranberries into a saucepan, find a comfortable seat somewhere, and pop them between your fingers. It's satisfying work. Don't worry if you miss some, but popping most of them open before you start will ensure your cordial is as strong and delicious as possible without having to boil it for too long.

2. Add the water to the saucepan, and bring to the boil over a moderate heat. Tip in the sugar and cinnamon sticks, and simmer gently for 15 minutes.

3. Add the lemon zest and juice, and simmer for a further 5 minutes.

4. Turn off the heat, and allow the cordial to sit and cool for 10 minutes. Strain through a clean piece of muslin, and pour into sterilized bottles.

The Christmas tree was ruled by an angel. She had a fine kingdom. It seemed to float, above its glossy mound of presents, a mist came off of it, the magical mingling of tinsel with fairy lights, of dust and pale daylight from the bay window, of faded olive-green foliage with many colours and forms of decorative bauble.

Ordinary People, Diana Evans

There have been many different Christmas trees in my life. As a child we were short on space, so Mum had to get creative. One year, she fixed a white bed sheet to the wall, a ribbon running down it in a zigzagged suggestion of a tree. A year later, she stripped twigs from the garden of their lush Australian summer leaves, sprayed them gold, and arranged them in a vase on the dining table. When my stepdad, Geoff, moved in, he brought a plastic tree with him that we clipped together and draped with tinsel each December. We replaced it, eventually, with a more sizeable one, but I have a soft spot for that first, small one he brought into our home.

These Christmas trees, though they filled me with an almost impossibly distracting level of joy, still paled in comparison to the sort of tree I longed to have in our house. I knew that it should be 'twice as tall as a boy' (from Truman Capote's *A Christmas Memory*), 'straight as a mast' (*The Dark is Rising* by Susan Cooper), and be covered in 'everything, and more' (Charles Dickens' *A Christmas Tree*). The promise of moving to England, where I could finally have a 'real' tree in my living room, was one I met with palpable excitement.

I spent my first London Christmas season in Whitechapel with three fellow Australians. Our flat had sash windows that allowed the winter cold to creep inside, and a tiny galley kitchen. One weekend in December, bundled up in scarves and coats, we bought a tree that promised to take up a decent chunk of our snug living room. We walked it home, hoisted onto our shoulders, and took an embarrassing number of photographs with it (none of us were used to buying a tree bound up in a string sack).

A few weeks later, I boarded a packed train due West, standing awkwardly among a crowd of people journeying back for the holidays. Arriving at my home away from home in a Cotswolds village, I was thrilled to discover that the family tree was not yet decorated – I was going to have two bites at the apple. I pulled decorations (ones that would become familiar in the years to come) from cardboard boxes, and hung them from the scented branches.

When I moved to Hackney, my flat was so tiny our Christmases there mandated little potted trees from Columbia Road Flower Market, which made our decorations look oversized and faintly ridiculous. Years later, as a nanny, I was thrilled by the size of the tree that fitted into the kitchen in Clapham – it was taller than me, and lush and rich. But it wasn't *mine*. That elusive perfect tree, the one I dreamed about, was still to come.

This year, for the first time since moving to England, I have a space of my own. I have a corner well suited to a tree, boxes of decorations, and an excessive length of fairy lights. The tree this year smells undeniably of Christmas – of warm pine and winter days – and it might, aesthetically, be my favourite ever. But, most importantly, the decorations that hang on it have some thirty years of history behind them, reminding me of all the trees/bed sheets/branches they have hung from in years past.

Spiced quince jelly

I read *The Owl and the Pussycat* at my dad's wedding when I was
eight, and have been taken with quinces and runcible spoons ever
since. Arriving as the year draws to a close, quinces demand a little
time and attention. Inedible when raw, the yellow skin and white
flesh turns a deep, gorgeous red once cooked. This jelly is wonderful
with cheese, on toast, or spooned over porridge or rice pudding
(save a jar for the Christmas Eve breakfast on p82).

FILLS 3 X 250ML/9OZ JARS

4 quinces
2 cinnamon sticks
2 star anise
Juice of 1 lemon

500g/2½ cups preserving sugar*

EQUIPMENT
A piece of muslin/cheesecloth

* You can use granulated sugar, as quinces have enough pectin to set the jelly, but
preserving sugar will make it easier to get a really clear jelly.

1. Wash the quinces, and roughly chop; remove any woody stems or
browned parts, but leave the skin and core. Place in a large saucepan.

2. Cover the fruit with cold water (at least 1 litre/4¼ cups), add the
cinnamon and star anise, and bring to a gentle simmer. Cover with a
lid, and leave to bubble gently for a couple of hours, until the fruit has
turned pink-red, and is soft and yielding.

3. Line a strainer with a piece of muslin, and place over a bowl. Pour
the fruit into it, and drain overnight; don't try to rush it and push the
fruit through or you will end up with a cloudy jelly.

4. The next day, place a plate in your freezer for testing the jelly. Add
the lemon juice to the strained quince juice, and then top up with
water until you have 600ml/2½ cups of liquid.

5. Pour into a saucepan and add the sugar. Bring to a slow boil, and skim off any white scum that rises to the surface with a wet spoon. After about 20 minutes (though you can start testing whenever you like – it's hard to give precise timings as it will depend on how fast you're boiling), turn off the heat. Spoon a small amount of the jelly onto the frozen plate, count to five, and draw your finger through it. If the liquid floods back into the line you have drawn, turn the heat back on and simmer for a bit longer. If the line remains clear, your jelly is ready.

6. Pour into sterilized jars, and place the lids on while the jelly is still hot. The texture of the jelly should fall somewhere between solid and liquid – a kind of quivering, viscous gel. Once cooled (it will continue to set as it cools), tip the jar and ensure that it has set to the desired consistency – you can pour the jelly back into the saucepan and simmer it gently for a couple more minutes if not.

Almond and pistachio biscotti

In *The Children of Green Knowe*, Tolly ensures everyone – human and animal – has a Christmas gift. The Christmas tree he readies for the birds, mice and rabbits is home to all manner of edible gifts: almonds, raisins, cheese, coconut. Though there's much to be enjoyed in a gift of cheese beneath the tree, if you want to do something a little 'more' with the almonds, these biscotti are just the thing.

MAKES 24

100g/¾ cup almonds
50g/½ cup shelled pistachios
300g/2¼ cups plain/all-purpose flour
200g/1 cup caster/superfine sugar
1tsp baking powder

½tsp fine salt
2–3 eggs
Zest of 2 clementines
1tbsp fennel seeds
50g/⅓ cup icing/confectioners' sugar

1. Preheat the oven to 220°C/425°F/Gas 7. Toast the nuts in a dry pan. Don't let them colour too much; you want them to take on a little gold.

2. Mix the flour, sugar, baking powder, and salt together in a large bowl. Beat two of the eggs with the clementine zest, and pour this in, mixing with a wooden spoon. Knead the dough, adding some of the third egg if it is too dry and crumbly. Mix in the nuts and fennel seeds.

3. Divide and shape the dough into two logs, and place on a baking sheet, at least 5cm/2in apart. Don't worry when they start to spread a little. Dust with icing sugar, and transfer to the oven for 25 minutes.

4. Once firm and cooked inside (a skewer will come out clean), remove from the oven, and reduce the heat to 180°C/350°F/Gas 4.

5. Allow the logs to cool a little, until you can just touch them, then cut into finger-width slices. Lay them out on a lined baking sheet, cut-side up. Bake for 15 minutes, then turn them over and give them a final 15 minutes. They should be crisp; perfect for dipping into coffee.

Crystallized ginger

A tin of crystallized ginger feels like a nod to a bygone era: to large country estates, and to hampers arriving from department stores on Christmas Eve. This is helped, at least in my head, by their presence in Agatha Christie's *The Adventure of the Christmas Pudding*, where they are part of an extravagant spread of 'old desserts' – sugar plums, almonds, and crystallized fruit.

MAKES AROUND 100 PIECES – PLENTY TO GO UNDER THE TREE

200g/7oz fresh ginger (peeled weight)
2tbsp honey
A pinch of salt

400g/2 cups golden caster/superfine sugar
Flavourless oil, for greasing

1. Slice the ginger into very thin discs and place in a small saucepan. Cover with water, then bring to a simmer over a medium heat and bubble away for 12 minutes. Strain off the cooking liquid, setting it aside for later, then cover the ginger with more water and simmer for a further 12 minutes. Strain the liquid, again retaining it for later.

2. Put the honey, salt and cooked ginger in a large saucepan along with 300g/1½ cups of the sugar and 375ml/generous 1½ cups of the cooking liquid. Bring to the boil, then simmer until the syrup resembles runny honey.

3. While the syrup is bubbling away, put out a wire/cooling rack with a lined baking sheet underneath to catch the drips. Rub the rack with a tiny amount of flavourless oil so the ginger doesn't stick. Place the remaining 100g/½ cup of sugar in a shallow bowl.

4. Remove the saucepan from the heat and set aside to cool slightly. Scoop the ginger out with a slotted spoon, drop the pieces into the sugar and toss to coat. Transfer to the wire rack and allow to dry for a

couple of hours, or overnight. Store in a jar or airtight container; the ginger will keep for a few weeks at room temperature. You can eat the pieces as they are, or chop them up and add them to biscuits, cookies, cakes or puddings.

NOTE: The ginger syrup you will have leftover in the saucepan at the end can be poured over ice cream or pancakes, or added to cakes. Any excess sugar is perfect for gingery baking.

Turkish delight

During Edmund's first visit to Narnia he finds himself wrapped in furs on the White Witch's sleigh. At this point in the story, of course, it is still always winter, but never Christmas. Yet, in spite of this, that image of the snow and the sleigh means that the squidgy pink squares of Turkish delight that she plies him with make most sense to me as a festive treat. To abandon your siblings in hopes of a kingship takes something pretty memorable; happily, Turkish delight delivers.

MAKES AROUND 30 SQUARES

450g/2¼ cups granulated sugar
1tbsp lemon juice
475ml/2 cups water
90g/¾ cup cornflour/cornstarch
½tsp cream of tartar
1tbsp rosewater
Pink food colouring (ideally paste)

TO DECORATE
40g/⅓ cup cornflour/cornstarch
40g/¼ cup icing/confectioners' sugar
Edible glitter (optional)

EQUIPMENT
Small, straight-sided baking pan (mine is 20x12cm/8x4¾in)

1. Place the sugar and lemon juice in a small saucepan with 175ml/¾ cup of the water. Put the pan over a medium-low heat and stir until the sugar has dissolved. Once the liquid is clear, stop stirring and heat until the sugar syrup reaches 118°C/245°F (around 15 minutes).

2. Line the baking pan with plastic wrap, smoothing the base and sides as much as possible. Sift the cornflour and cream of tartar into a saucepan, along with the remaining 300ml/1¼ cups of water. Place over a low heat and stir continuously. The mixture will start to thicken. Keep cooking it until it resembles hair gel – thick and gloopy.

3. Stirring constantly, slowly pour in the hot sugar syrup. Continue to stir over a low heat for around an hour. The mixture will look strange

(and separated) at first, but it will come together. When it's done, it will have taken on a golden tinge and be very thick and difficult to stir. I know this is a long time to keep stirring, but I find it soothing – it's something you can do with a Christmas film playing.

4. Remove from the heat and beat in the rosewater and food colouring. Scoop the Turkish delight into the lined baking pan – this will be messy. Smooth the top with a wet spatula and push down. Cover with a tea towel and allow it to set overnight in a cool room.

5. The next day, turn the Turkish delight out of the pan and peel off the plastic wrap. Wet a knife with hot water and slice into squares. To decorate, sift the cornflour and icing sugar into a shallow bowl (along with the edible glitter if you're using it). Drop the squares into the bowl and toss to coat each piece. Gift it as soon as you can after this (or add a little extra cornflour to the box before you do), as the damp squares of Turkish delight will eventually soak up the powder. Store in a cool, dry place, with greaseproof/wax paper between the layers.

French bonbons

On the first Christmas morning we see in *Little Women*, the March sisters descend the stairs and are met with a glorious breakfast spread: Buckwheats! Muffins! Cream! In the end though, they walk through snowy Concord to take it to the Hummels. Late on Christmas evening, Mr Laurence ensures that their day is not devoid of gastronomic treats – the ice cream, cake and bonbons he sends are the first they've seen since the war began. We may not be experiencing Civil War rationing, but a small box of these is still ideal for someone you really wish to impress. If you're put off by the idea of chocolate moulds and tempering, you can make a much easier version: teaspoons of the ganache shaped into balls and rolled in cocoa powder would be just as welcome.

MAKES 30 CHOCOLATES

GANACHE FILLING
150ml/⅔ cup double/heavy cream
½tsp ground cinnamon
Zest of 2 clementines
150g/5½oz dark/bittersweet chocolate
(at least 70% cocoa), chopped
2tbsp Armagnac
6 prunes

TEMPERED SHELLS (OPTIONAL)
300g/10½oz dark/bittersweet chocolate
(at least 70% cocoa), chopped

EQUIPMENT
Thermometer
Chocolate moulds (I find that silicone
works best)
Piping bag

1. Put the cream in a small saucepan with the cinnamon and clementine zest. Place over a low heat until almost simmering. Remove from the heat and pour over the chocolate for the filling.

2. Put the Armagnac and prunes in another saucepan, and place over a low heat. Bring almost to the boil, then take off the heat and allow to stand for 5 minutes. Pour the Armagnac into the chocolate ganache,

then finely dice the prunes and fold through carefully. Set the ganache aside to cool.

3. Next, temper the chocolate for the shells. Place two-thirds of this chocolate in a heatproof bowl over a pan of barely simmering water, ensuring that the water doesn't ever touch the bowl directly. Stir while it melts, keeping the heat as low as you can. Once the chocolate has melted, pay close attention and remove it from the heat once it has reached 52°C/126°F. Wrap the base of the bowl in a tea towel to keep it warm, and stir in the remaining third of the chocolate. Once melted, continue to stir until the temperature reduces to 32°C/90°F.

4. Use a plastic spoon (a metal one will cool the chocolate too quickly) to transfer small amounts of the chocolate into each mould, and push it around until it covers the base and sides. Add more if you can still see the light through the chocolate when you hold it up to a window. Leave to set.

5. Spoon the ganache into a piping bag and pipe a little into each mould, ensuring that you leave space at the top for another layer of chocolate.

6. If your tempered chocolate has solidified, temper it again, following the same procedure as before. Remember to remove a third of it from the bowl, to add to the melted chocolate once you take it off the heat. With the plastic spoon, fill each chocolate mould up to the top. If you have dribbled chocolate over the silicone (I can't do this without getting it very messy), run a chocolate scraper or knife along the top of each chocolate to create a smooth finish.

7. Leave to set, but don't refrigerate, then carefully pop each bonbon out of its mould. Keep in a cool, dry place and consume within a couple of days.

On one side was a table occupied by some chattering girls, cutting up silk and gold paper; and on the other were tressels and trays, bending under the weight of brawn and cold pies, where riotous boys were holding high revel; the whole completed by a roaring Christmas fire, which seemed determined to be heard in spite of all the noise of the others.

Persuasion, Jane Austen

I moved to my old flat in Hackney on a grey November day in 2010. It was a cold winter, and a tricky one – the visceral joy I had felt during my first winter in the UK seemed impossible to grasp hold of, and a London sabbatical my dad had been on for six months was drawing swiftly to a close; he was soon to return to Australia. Desperately homesick, I felt lost and at sea. I longed for England to feel like home, to embrace Christmas and luxuriate in it, but I couldn't seem to drum up any excitement.

One Sunday afternoon, a week before Christmas, I sat on my living room floor, and put a copy of *The Sound of Music* into my laptop. Despite the summer setting (and the Nazis) *The Sound of Music* has always felt like a festive film to me; as kids my sister Lucy and I would watch it on repeat, as we wrote cards and wrapped presents. With the snow falling softly outside my window, I started wrapping gifts in brown paper and string, and felt a bit of the joy and wonder return. I Skyped Lucy, and we watched our favourite bits of the film together, reminiscing about Christmases we had shared. Later, with my sister asleep on the other side of the world, I turned to a veritable classic: *The Muppet Christmas Carol*, and my ultimate low-pressure, high-comfort supper (a cheese toastie, and tinned tomato soup). The season was still a tricky one, but rewatching the old familiar films helped make things feel okay for a while.

In the houses I was raised in, we have film-watching rituals down to a fine art. I grew up surrounded by books, certainly, but perhaps even more so by cinema: Saturday night comedies and adventure fantasy with Dad and Cheryl, and Sunday afternoon musicals and old classics at Mum and Geoff's. Lucy and I would watch our favourites so often that I can still tell you what commercials fall after each scene on our taped-off-television VHS collection. At Christmastime, with everyone off work, we'd ensconce ourselves on the sofas (or sit directly on the cool tiles if the heat was unbearable), and watch an annual succession of old favourites: *Home Alone, Die Hard, Little Women, It's a Wonderful Life, Holiday Inn, Bridget Jones's Diary.*

Like an uncontrollable Pavlovian response, a decade after that tricky Christmas in 2010, familiar Christmas films still work to kick-start my enthusiasm for the season. I feel instantly comforted, cosseted, and Christmassy on hearing the first bars of Thomas Newman's *Little Women* score, or the familiar sound of wind rushing through the Alps in the opening scene of *The Sound of Music*, or when I see the chimney pots of Victorian London at the beginning of *The Muppet Christmas Carol*. When I am feeling far from home, they provide a connection to family on the other side of the world, and a link to Christmases past.

My proper favourite of these, the one I watch multiple times every year without fail, is *The Muppet Christmas Carol*. I appreciate that in this book about books, I should be lending my voice to the 'read Dickens' *A Christmas Carol*' chorus. And you should! It's wonderful. But, knowing that I am here among friends and fans of Christmas,

I can tell you with utter sincerity that the film is, unquestionably, better than the book. Michael Caine, who spends the vast majority of his time onscreen interacting with a series of hands covered in fabric and googly eyes, deserved an Academy Award. He took the role under the proviso that he would not be asked to wink towards the camera; he wanted his performance as Ebenezer Scrooge to be taken entirely seriously. It shows. He oozes sincerity, and I am always wholeheartedly convinced by his transformation from miserly Tory to the most generous man in town. The surprise and unmasked affection on his face when Beaker hands him a red scarf at the end of the film makes me weep without fail. And he's just one part. I love having Gonzo onscreen in the role of Dickens himself. I love everything about Rizzo the Rat's presence. I love the music: a relentless and yet strangely welcome earworm, the Ghost of Christmas Present singing 'It Feels Like Christmas' enters my head in early December each year and refuses to leave until January.

Happily, my love for this film is neither unusual nor unique. Cinemas across the country host multiple screenings every December, so each year I find myself in among a sea of people in costumes or Christmas jumpers feeling a frisson of excitement when Kermit reassures us that it's only 'One More Sleep 'til Christmas'. It's a seasonal ritual now; one that feels inescapably part of my life here in England, but one that also contains a vital thread back to my family in Australia.

LET'S
PARTY
LIKE IT'S
1843

There were more dances, and there were forfeits, and more dances, and there was cake, and there was negus, and there was a great piece of Cold Roast, and there was a great piece of Cold Boiled, and there were mince-pies, and plenty of beer.

A Christmas Carol, Charles Dickens

Though I appreciate that they're not always the height of the social calendar, I have a deep affection for office Christmas parties. I know that, for many, they're slightly odd evenings in front of a set menu or supermarket sausage rolls, with an awkward Secret Santa that no one really wants to participate in, and a bunch of colleagues you wouldn't necessarily choose to drink with at 3 p.m. on a Tuesday. But, as with so much at this time of year, leaning in is the key.

I am aware that I may be spoilt by my experience. My first office Christmas party was hosted by my mum; I handed food and drinks around in her physiotherapy practice (where I 'worked' on reception), quietly sampling the Champagne and cheese with my sister, while we pretended to be terribly grown up. The first ones in England happened in theatres, where I loved my colleagues, and where the 11 p.m. karaoke was always startlingly impressive. I'm even more spoilt now that my 'office Christmas party' is just me and my best pal and catering partner Liv (and often Liv's husband Sam) going out for dumplings or steak and a few beers, while very deliberately not discussing the long list of weddings we'll be catering the next year. I realize I have been lucky. But if you're not quite so lucky, don't despair. Even a bad office party is a chance to get to know a colleague who works in another part of the building or, at the very least, an afternoon where no one is emailing you about payroll.

Of course, if the office Christmas party leaves you cold (or, as a freelancer or a student or a retiree or a remote worker, is missing from your calendar), you can always host your own. I often find myself hoping for an opportunity to get a group of my friends together before the year draws to a close, or we all head 'home' for Christmas. A sit-down dinner can feel like too much effort, or require space you simply don't have. But a drinks party that people can drop into, with some good music playing, bowls of your favourite crisps scattered about, and a couple of plates of whatever food you have found time to prepare, is the perfect sort of big group gathering at this time of year.

In terms of food, stuff that's easy to pick up with one hand is ideal; try to avoid something that's going to fall apart and destroy your carpet the minute someone bites into it. I have yet to make a crisp, fried thing that people haven't adored, which is why there are plenty of those on the pages that follow. Similarly (unsurprisingly) carbs are key – if you're only picking at a handful of things over the course of an evening, you want something that fills you up. I quite like being able to retreat into the kitchen during a party to fuss about a bit and have a breather. If that isn't your vibe, the ginger beer ham and buns, the not-sausage rolls, and the brownies and mince pies can all be prepared and plated when people walk through the door. Alternatively, keep it simple and throw a party like the one Carol and Therese skip in *Carol*: the Kellys' wine and fruitcake party (my dream, quite honestly). There's a recipe that starts on p139 that will help, should this appeal.

I hope the suggestions in the pages that follow aid you. And if in doubt, for the perfect Christmas party recipe, follow Fezziwig's lead in *A Christmas Carol* – plenty of dancing (though only in socked feet in my flat: wooden floors and downstairs neighbours are not a good mix), games, drinks, cake, cold meat, and mince pies.

Champagne cocktails

In Nancy Mitford's *Christmas Pudding*, Paul Fotheringay
(masquerading for the season under the name Fisher) suggests
some 'economical' Champagne cocktails – the cheapest Champagne,
a little brandy, and some sugar – for a party, with the promise
that 'people do seem to like them most awfully'. His suggestion
is rebuffed by Lady Bobbin, who is convinced that a cocktail
habit is a 'pernicious and disgusting' one. I am, unsurprisingly,
wholeheartedly on Paul F.'s side.

You can, of course, find delicious crémant, cava and other fizzy
wine at a very reasonable price in supermarkets and off-licences,
which will be lovely on its own. But if you fancy making an average
bottle a little more special, there are plenty of ways to make that
happen. And there's a lot of fun to be had in setting up a makeshift
bar in a corner somewhere with a couple of options that people can
assemble themselves.

Sugar syrup (in advance)

200g/1 cup caster/superfine sugar   100ml/7tbsp water

Dissolve the sugar in the water over a low heat. Allow to cool, bottle,
and then store in the fridge.

One for Paul F.

A sugar cube   1tbsp Cognac or other brandy
6 drops Angostura bitters   Fizzy wine

Place the sugar cube in the bottom of a glass, and shake the bitters
onto it. Cover with Cognac, and then top up the glass with fizzy wine.

French 75

1tbsp lemon juice
1tsp sugar syrup

2tbsp gin
Fizzy wine

Shake the lemon juice, sugar syrup, and gin together with a couple of ice cubes. Strain into a glass and top up with fizzy wine.

Sparkling sherry

2tbsp sherry
1tsp juice from a jar of cherries

1 Maraschino cherry
Fizzy wine

Mix the sherry and cherry juice together in the bottom of a glass. Drop the cherry in, and top up with fizz.

Liqueur cocktails

Crème de cassis (a kir royale)
Sloe gin (a sloe royale)

Campari (an aperitivo spritz)
Fizzy wine

A tablespoon of spirit/liqueur in the bottom of a nice glass is the simplest way to zhuzh up a lackluster bottle. The two will combine better if you start with the liqueur and then slowly add your fizz.

Fruit cocktails

Fruit juice (pear, orange, peach, apple)
Soft fruit

Cordials (elderflower, cranberry)
Fizzy wine

Add fruit juice to Champagne at a ratio of 1:2 (one part juice, two parts fizz), crush some soft fruit in the glass, or add a tablespoon of cordial to the bottom of a glass before topping it up. An ideal option for brunch/lunch.

Latkes with apple sauce or spiced mayonnaise

My friend Fiona, who lives in Paris, always has a jar of duck fat in her fridge. Perhaps this is standard in her city (I like to imagine that it is), but regardless, when I asked her to show me how she makes latkes, she began by pulling out a jar of it. She told me that her grandma would make them with whatever was to hand – any kind of potato, any kind of flour, any kind of fat. Frying them in oil is most traditional, as it honours Hanukkah, when one cruse of oil miraculously lasted for eight days. But Fiona reckons that duck fat makes the best latkes possible. I am inclined to agree with her.

MAKES 40ISH LITTLE LATKES

LATKES
500g/1lb 2oz unpeeled waxy potatoes
1 small onion
1 egg
3tbsp plain/all-purpose flour
Salt and black pepper
3tbsp duck fat, or oil with a high
  smoking point

APPLE SAUCE
1 cooking apple
1tsp lemon juice (optional)

SPICED MAYONNAISE
3tbsp mayonnaise
1tsp lemon juice
¼tsp smoked paprika

TO SERVE
Sour cream
Finely chopped chives

EQUIPMENT
A piece of muslin/cheesecloth*

* You can drain the grated potato through a fine sieve or strainer, if you don't have a piece of muslin or cheesecloth, but nothing will get the water out of it quite as efficiently. I have a collection of those posh face cloths you often end up with for this purpose; they do absolutely nothing for my skin but plenty for my cooking.

1. Grate the potatoes on a coarse box grater, and then put the strands in a piece of muslin and squeeze until it stops releasing water. It will take a little while; there is a lot of water in potato, and the drier you

can get it, the crisper your latkes will be. Leave to drain while you make the apple sauce.

2. Peel and chop the apple, and place it in a saucepan with a splash of water. Cook until it collapses entirely and forms a sauce, adding a splash more water if it is too dry. Taste and add some lemon juice if the apple is too sweet.

3. If you'd prefer the latkes with mayonnaise (I do, sometimes), season the mayo with the lemon and paprika and set aside.

4. Put the drained potato in a bowl. Peel the onion and grate it over the potato. Crack in the egg, and then add the flour. Bring the mixture together with a wooden spoon; if it doesn't hold together, add a little more flour. Season generously.

5. Warm the duck fat in a frying pan over a moderate heat. Take small pinches of the potato mixture, just less than a tablespoon, and squash them together into little cakes. Fry for a couple of minutes on each side, until golden brown, and then drain on paper towels.

6. Top the warm latkes with the mayonnaise, or the apple sauce, and a dab of sour cream, and then finish with a pinch of chopped chives.

Ginger beer ham on brioche buns

The Great Gatsby truly couldn't be less of a Christmas book, set as it is over a long, hot summer in New York and on Long Island. And yet, when I think of cocktail parties, I think of Jay Gatsby's well-attended extravaganzas. He's miserable throughout, of course, but his guests have a roaring time – thanks in no small part to the lavish spread he puts on. Little rolls and piles of sliced meat always go down well. You could also serve this ham whole on Christmas Day – with or without the rolls.

MAKES 24 LITTLE ROLLS

BRIOCHE BUNS
150ml/⅔ cup milk
150ml/⅔ cup water
25g/1½tbsp fresh yeast (or 7g/1½tsp fast-action yeast)
2tbsp caster/superfine sugar
1 egg, plus 1 beaten egg, to glaze
250g/1¾ cups + 2tbsp plain/all-purpose flour
250g/1¾ cups strong bread flour
A pinch of salt
50g/3½tbsp butter, softened
30g/¼ cup sesame seeds

HAM
2 onions
1.2kg/2lb 10oz rolled pork shoulder
1¼ litres/5½ cups ginger beer
2tbsp seeded mustard
2tbsp golden syrup

TO SERVE
Butter
Chilli jam

1. First, make the brioche rolls. Warm the milk and water in a pan over the stove. When they're at room temperature, whisk in the yeast. Add the sugar, and the egg. Combine the flours and salt in a bowl, and pour in the wet ingredients. Bring it together with your hands, and knead the dough by hand or in a mixer until smooth, elastic, and no longer sticky. Knead in the butter, a small piece at a time. Put the dough in a clean bowl, cover, and leave to double in size; it should take an hour or two, depending on how cold your kitchen is.

2. While the dough is rising, start on the ham. Peel the onions, slice them in half, and place in a large saucepan along with the ham. Pour over the ginger beer and bring to the boil over a moderate heat. Reduce to a gentle simmer, and cover the pan with foil or a lid so that the liquid doesn't boil off. Simmer for an hour and a half.

3. Once the dough has risen, divide it into 24 evenly sized pieces. Shape each into a ball, folding the dough underneath, and then rolling it on the work surface. Place the buns on a baking sheet lined with parchment paper, spacing them 2cm/¾in apart. Cover with a tea towel and leave to rise again; they should bounce back when you prod them, and will have increased a little in size.

4. Preheat the oven to 220°C/425°F/Gas 7. Paint the buns with the beaten egg, then sprinkle with sesame seeds. Bake for 15 minutes, until risen, and golden brown.

5. Turn the oven up to 240°C/475°F/Gas 8. Take the ham out of the ginger beer, and snip away any string holding it together. Score a deep crosshatch into the fat, and place the ham in a small roasting pan, or wrap the base with foil, so there is as little space as possible for the golden syrup to escape and burn. Whisk together the mustard and golden syrup, and spoon it over the ham. Roast in the oven for 15–20 minutes. Do keep an eye on it, as the syrup can burn quickly.

6. Leave the ham to cool a little, and then slice thinly. Split open the buns, spread with a little butter and chilli jam, and stuff with the ham. Serve warm or cold.

Crab cakes

I associate fancy seafood and shellfish with Christmas in Australia. My stepmother's dad would haul up pots of crab during the summer when we went to visit, especially around Christmas. If you are lucky enough to have fresh crabmeat, I suggest eating it simply with some good white or brown bread, butter, and lemon. But out of season, and year-round, a tin of crabmeat can be employed to make some delicious finger food.

MAKES 30 LITTLE FISH CAKES

CRAB CAKES
300g/10½oz Maris Piper potatoes
300g/10½oz tinned white crabmeat
2 spring onions/scallions, finely sliced
Zest of 1 lemon
2 eggs
10g/½ cup chopped dill
15g/¾ cup chopped tarragon
20g/1 cup chopped parsley
3tbsp capers, chopped
Salt and black pepper

TO COOK
50g/heaped ⅓ cup plain/all-purpose flour
2 eggs, beaten
125g/1½ cups dried white breadcrumbs
150ml/⅔ cup groundnut or vegetable oil

TO SERVE
1 lemon
Flaky sea salt
Mayonnaise and/or chilli sauce

1. Peel and chop the potatoes into chunks. Place in a pan, cover with cold water, and bring to the boil. Simmer for 15 minutes, until soft. Drain, then press through a potato ricer, or mash in a bowl.

2. Mix the crabmeat, spring onions, and lemon zest through the potato. Crack the eggs and beat with a fork, then mix them in too. Add the chopped herbs and capers, and season.

3. Form into small balls, around the size of a walnut in its shell. Flatten a little, and place on a baking sheet. Put the sheet in the freezer for 15 minutes, or in the fridge for an hour if that's easier.

4. Set up a little production line to cook the crab cakes. Fill a bowl with the flour, another with the beaten eggs, and a third with the breadcrumbs. Cover the crab cakes in flour, dip them in the egg, and then dredge in breadcrumbs. Place on a second baking sheet until you've prepped the whole batch.

5. Warm the oil in a frying pan over a moderate heat and, once hot, carefully place the crab cakes into it in batches. Once they're golden brown underneath, flip them over, and allow to cook on the other side. Drain on paper towels, then give them a little squeeze of lemon and a few flakes of sea salt on top. Serve warm, with mayonnaise or chilli sauce, for dipping.

Porcini mushroom arancini

In terms of crowd-pleasing party food, there is little better you can offer than arancini. These rich mushroom ones, with stringy mozzarella, are a version Liv and I have been making for years – in their many hundreds. Unless your kitchen is closed off from guests (all my living space is in one room), I recommend frying the arancini before anyone arrives, and then keeping them warm and crisp in a low oven; hot oil is not something you want to be dealing with once people are running in and out, or when you have a drink in your hand.

MAKES 24 ARANCINI

ARANCINI
10g/⅓ cup dried porcini mushrooms
1tbsp oil
1tbsp butter
2 brown onions, diced
4 cloves garlic, finely chopped
300g/scant 1½ cups arborio rice
Up to 800ml/3½ cups mushroom or
    vegetable stock, warmed

125g/2 cups chestnut/cremini
    mushrooms, finely diced
Salt and black pepper
2 balls mozzarella, diced

FOR COOKING
50g/heaped ⅓ cup flour
1 egg, beaten
80g/2 cups panko breadcrumbs
2 litres/8¾ cups vegetable oil

1. Rehydrate the porcini mushrooms by covering them with boiling water. Leave for 20 minutes, then drain and chop, reserving the water.

2. Heat the oil and butter in large pan. Cook the onions until translucent, then add the garlic and cook for a few minutes. Add the rice and stir through the onions. Pour in the porcini mushroom liquid and stir as it bubbles away, then start adding the warm stock, a ladleful at a time. After about 10 minutes, add the chopped fresh and porcini mushrooms. Keep adding stock until the rice is cooked through, with no chalky interior. Taste, and season with salt and

pepper. Allow to cool, then fold in the mozzarella, and refrigerate until cold.

3. Roll the chilled risotto into ping-pong-sized balls. Set up an assembly line to coat the balls. Dip each arancini first into the flour, then into the beaten egg, then into the panko breadcrumbs.

4. Heat the vegetable oil in a large, deep pan to 180°C/355°F. Cook the arancini in small batches, submerging them in the oil until golden. Drain on paper towels, and sprinkle with flaky sea salt before serving alongside a sauce made from chopped capers, shallots, parsley, and a little red wine vinegar, or some pesto, or mayonnaise.

5:30 a.m. Why hasn't Rebecca invited me to her party? Why? Why? How many more parties are going on that everyone has been invited to except me? I bet everyone is at one now, laughing and sipping expensive Champagne. No one likes me. Christmas is going to be a total party-desert…

Bridget Jones's Diary, Helen Fielding

The tricky thing about Christmas and New Year's Eve is that everything is supposed to be warm and lovely and twinkly. This time of year is *supposed* to be filled with love and joy and kin. The season is so easy to romanticize (you're holding a book focused mainly on just how glorious it can be!), but the inevitable reality is that, often, it is far from perfect. For so many possible reasons – money, strained relationships, difficult anniversaries, a snap election – this can be a tough time of year.

Though I generally sail through December like the Ghost of Christmas Present, light of spirit and full of love for the season and all that it offers, there have been years where I have struggled. I've spent time trapped under anxiety, triggered by the arrival of the beginning of a new year, and all that I thought I could/should/would have achieved. Despite being lucky in my friendships and my families, I have spent Christmases overwhelmed by loneliness – whether literally alone or in the company of others.

In the face of parties and events, I have plastered a smile on my face that in no way reflected how I was feeling. It is so easy to look at Christmas and imagine that the lights, the relentlessly jolly music, the general cheer, might have a resoundingly positive effect. In reality, these seasonal markers, these constant tiny rituals, can instead serve to remind us of what has been lost. So, if you are approaching Christmas this year with a sense of dread, know that I wish I was there to put a comforting hand on your shoulder. Know too that you are very, very much not alone.

I will almost always turn to time in the kitchen when seeking comfort – I want the reassurance of flour between my fingertips as I make pastry, the smell of a chicken roasting in the oven, the taste of melted butter that's run through a crumpet and down my wrist. But sometimes even making something delicious to eat feels like too much emotional pressure. When it is the shadow of the familiar that causes the ache, time in the kitchen with old favourites only serves to remind me why I am finding things so hard.

I don't know what has the potential to work for you, but I have found the following invaluable to remember in tricky years. If the thought of carrying on as you have in years past is too difficult, take some time to establish new rituals. Visit new places, see new people, watch new films, cook new food. I have found it reassuring to remember that though this is a period of love, joy and kin, it is also a time for rest. It is entirely appropriate to cut corners if you are entertaining; to buy a bunch of reduced price canapés and oven chips on Christmas Eve (either in company or on your own), and spend Christmas watching an array of gloriously terrible films. The joy of some 5,000 years of solstice and, later, Christmas traditions is that there are no rules – you can make the season into anything that will work for you.

Not-sausage rolls

In D. H. Lawrence's *Sons and Lovers*, he describes the Christmas scene that awaits William on his arrival home: a roaring fire, and 'a scent of cooked pastry'. An instant welcome. It helps, of course, that there are very few pastry-based things – pies, tarts, sausage rolls, fancy desserts – you could pull from an oven that I wouldn't be thrilled by. I am loath to pick favourites, but very rare months go by without my making sausage rolls for one event or another. They're the definition of a crowd pleaser, either in their original pork form (recipe in *The Little Library Cookbook*) or this deeply savoury vegan-friendly version.

MAKES 16 SMALL OR 4 LARGE ROLLS

1 medium leek, finely diced
2tbsp groundnut or vegetable oil
200g/7oz chestnut/cremini mushrooms, finely diced
1tbsp soy sauce
1tbsp mirin
1tbsp brown miso paste
125g/4½oz frozen spinach
Generous pinch of white pepper

A pinch of togarashi (optional – it's a little spicy)
100g/1¾ cups soft breadcrumbs
250g/9oz puff pastry (most supermarket ones are vegan, but do read the packaging)
2tbsp oat milk
2tsp sesame seeds (mix of black and white)

1. Fry the leek until soft in a tablespoon of the oil over a moderate heat. Transfer to a bowl, and then fry the mushrooms in the rest of the oil. Keep cooking until the water released by the mushrooms has evaporated, and the pan is dry.

2. Return the leeks to the pan, and add the soy, mirin, miso paste and spinach. Cook until the mixture dries out. Taste, and season with white pepper (it probably won't need salt, thanks to the soy, but do add it if it needs it). Add the togarashi, if you're using it. Remove from

the heat and stir in the breadcrumbs. Chill the mixture completely in the fridge.

3. Preheat the oven to 200°C/400°F/Gas 6. Roll out the pastry into a rectangle, about 50cm/20in long, and 20cm/8in wide. Distribute the filling along one of the long edges, paint the opposite edge with a little of the oat milk (to help seal) and roll tightly. Arrange so the seal is underneath.

4. Paint the top with the remaining oat milk, and slice into 16 small or 4 large rolls. Transfer onto a baking sheet lined with baking parchment, make small slashes in the top of each roll, and sprinkle with the sesame seeds. Bake for 30 minutes, until the pastry has flaked and is a rich golden brown.

Greens for sustenance

It would be disingenuous of me to suggest that I'd be comfortable with a December that was one long perpetual party. When things get busy towards the end of the year, I deliberately carve out evenings to spend in my own company. This, then, is a dinner for that eventual, blissful night in. Not too complicated, and filled with greens – just what I crave after multiple nights of mince pies and mulled wine.

Serves 1

4 leaves cavolo nero
1 small bunch spring/collard greens
2tsp sesame oil
60g/2oz dried buckwheat noodles
1tsp soy sauce
1tsp hoisin sauce
1tsp chilli sauce (I like Laoganma)
1 egg
1 spring onion/scallion, finely sliced
1tsp black sesame seeds

1. Chop the woody stems out of the greens and slice the leaves into ribbons. Warm a heavy-based frying pan over a low heat, pour in a teaspoon of the oil, and add the greens. Keep them moving until crisp in places and cooked through, while you get on with the rest of the meal.

2. Bring a saucepan of salted water to the boil, and simmer the noodles until tender.

3. Meanwhile, mix the soy, hoisin, and chilli sauces together in a bowl. Once the noodles are tender, drain well, and add back to the saucepan, stirring the sauce through them.

4. Remove the greens from the frying pan, toss through the noodles, and keep warm over a very low heat. Turn the heat up underneath the frying pan. Pour in the remaining teaspoon of sesame oil, and crack the egg into the oil. Pop a lid on for a minute while the egg fries.

5. Tip the noodles and greens into a bowl, and then put the egg on top. Finish with finely sliced spring onions and the sesame seeds.

Mince pies

Is it really even December if you've not yet had a mince pie? Inextricably linked to the season, there are few books featuring Christmas that don't mention mince pies somewhere – Samuel Pepys has one on Christmas night, and they're in eaten in *Jane Eyre* (though these would have had included mutton, beef, or even goose), in Kate Atkinson's *Behind the Scenes at the Museum*, and by the Starkadders in *Christmas at Cold Comfort Farm*. The first place I remember seeing them was in *The Jolly Christmas Postman*; the Wolf is pulling crackers with our titular hero, and 'wolfing' pies and sherry. A truly iconic combination. I have been making these for years – they started out as Nigella's, but have been tweaked over the years so as to remind me more of mum's mince pies back home.

MAKES 24

MINCEMEAT
75ml/5tbsp Port wine
75g/6tbsp dark brown sugar
1tsp ground ginger
½tsp ground cloves
1tsp ground cinnamon
2 small apples, unpeeled, grated
150g/1 cup sultanas/golden raisins
150g/1 cup raisins
50g/scant ½ cup dried cranberries
Zest and juice of 2 clementines

1tsp vanilla extract
½tsp almond extract
2tbsp honey

PASTRY
180g/¾ cup + 2tsp butter, cubed
360g/2¾ cups plain/all-purpose flour
Zest and juice of 2 clementines
A pinch of salt
Icing/confectioners' sugar, to decorate

1. To make the mincemeat, warm the Port and brown sugar in a saucepan over a low heat, swirling until the sugar dissolves. Add the spices, grated apple and dried fruit, along with the zest and juice of the clementines. Cook for around 20 minutes over a medium heat, stirring every so often to ensure the mixture isn't sticking. Once the liquid has reduced, turn off the heat and add the vanilla and almond

extracts and the honey. Beat well. Transfer the mixture to jars (which makes a lovely gift) or an airtight container. This will keep for a good few months, but can also be used the same day (once cool).

2. To make the pastry, toss the butter through the flour and put the whole lot in the freezer for 20 minutes. Place the clementine zest and juice into a glass with the pinch of salt, and chill in the fridge. Remove the flour mix from the freezer and blitz in a food processor until it resembles breadcrumbs (this can be done by hand if you like; just skip the freezer step, using cold butter from the fridge instead, and rub the mixture between your fingers until it resembles breadcrumbs). Slowly dribble in the clementine juice and zest, stopping when the pastry comes together. If you need more liquid, add some chilled water. Tip the pastry out, squidge into a ball, cover in plastic wrap and chill for at least 1 hour.

3. Preheat the oven to 190°C/375°F/Gas 5. Cut the pastry into quarters, storing it in the fridge until needed. Roll each piece out to the thickness of a pound coin between two sheets of greaseproof/wax paper. Cut fluted circles and stars out of the pastry, bringing it back together and rolling out again to use it all. Push each pastry circle into a greased muffin cup, fill with a tablespoon of the mincemeat and top with a pastry star. Don't fill them right to the brim, as they'll bubble up and spill over.

4. Bake for 15 minutes, or until golden brown. Allow the tarts to cool a little in the pan, then push one edge (lightly – you don't want to break the pastry) and the tart should pop out. Place on a wire/cooling rack and, once completely cool, dust with icing sugar.

Cherry and pecan brownies

Last December, I made some snacks for one of my favourite bookshops, the London Review Bookshop, to hand around on one of their Christmas evenings. They are lovely nights – people wander about with wine, doing their shopping, and having books signed. To tempt, the food needs to be crowd-pleasing, easy to eat with one hand, and good enough that you'd put up with juggling an armful of books and a full glass to eat it anyway. Brownies (alongside sausage rolls) seemed like a logical choice – as they do at any party. These ones are filled with some Christmas spices and – because for some reason a Black Forest gateau feels impossibly Christmassy – kirsch-soaked cherries.

SERVES 12–16

CHERRIES
200g/7oz pitted cherries (at this time of year, look for frozen ones)
2tbsp kirsch (or Port)
2tsp mixed spice
Zest of 2 oranges

BROWNIES
300g/10½oz dark/bittersweet chocolate
250g/1 cup + 2tbsp butter

150g/¾ cup light brown sugar
150g/¾ cup golden caster/superfine sugar
4 eggs
75g/¾ cup pecans
60g/½ cup plain/all-purpose flour
60g/½ cup cocoa powder
½tsp baking powder
A generous pinch of sea salt

1. Preheat your oven to 170°C/325°F/Gas 3. Butter and line a 25cm/10in square baking pan with parchment paper; a brownie will be too delicate to 'turn out', so you will need plenty of paper overhanging to grasp hold of once it's baked.

2. Put the cherries in a small saucepan with the kirsch and mixed spice. Bring to a simmer on the hob, reduce the liquid by half (keep moving the cherries around so they don't burn), and then remove

from the heat. Add the orange zest, and set aside while you make the brownie batter.

3. Place a heatproof bowl on top of a pan of simmering water (making sure the water does not touch the bottom of the bowl) and melt 200g/7oz of the chocolate, along with the butter. Remove from the heat and beat in the sugars until the mixture is smooth. Crack in the eggs, one at a time, and beat to combine.

4. Roughly chop the pecans and the remaining chocolate, and fold them through, along with the cherries and their syrupy liquid. Sift the flour, cocoa, and baking powder into the mixture and fold in with a spatula until just combined. Do this gently, but make sure you get rid of any white streaks.

5. Pour the mixture into the pan, then smooth out the top. Bake in the oven for 40 minutes. After this time, the batter will have risen a little, and will have stopped wobbling enthusiastically in the middle. Remove from the oven when a skewer inserted comes out sticky, but without raw dough on it. Start checking the brownies after around 30 minutes, and err on the side of caution; you can always pop it back into the oven for a minute or so, but you can't reclaim the dense fudginess the middle of a brownie should have. Sprinkle with the salt, and leave to cool in the pan before cutting into squares.

Eggnog

If you've only seen the eggnog that is poured from a carton in American sitcoms, then you are in for a treat. This is pure Christmas: essentially spiced and/or boozy custard that you can pour into a fancy glass and get away with claiming as a reasonable drink. What a joy this season is. It's what Moominmamma makes for the Moomins when they wake up early one year and are confused by Christmas rituals in *The Fir Tree*. I promise, it will be just as welcome beside your Christmas tree too.

MAKES 4 SMALL GLASSES

225ml/scant 1 cup whole milk
75ml/⅓ cup double/heavy cream
¼tsp ground mace
½tsp ground nutmeg, plus extra to serve

½tsp ground cinnamon
2 eggs, separated
1tbsp caster/superfine sugar
100ml/scant ½ cup bourbon (optional)

1. Bring the milk, cream, and spices to a slow simmer over a low heat. Meanwhile, whisk the egg yolks and sugar for a couple of minutes in a bowl, until very pale, and forming thick ribbons when dropped from the whisk.

2. Pour the simmering milk over the yolks, whisking constantly to prevent them scrambling, and then add the bourbon, if you're using it. Cover, and put the bowl in the fridge, to chill the mixture. If you're including the bourbon, leave for 24 hours (or up to 3 days) to allow the flavours to develop. Either way, don't forget to hold onto the egg whites – you'll need them too.

3. When you're ready to serve, beat the egg whites to soft peaks. Carefully fold into the cold eggnog mixture, then pour into glasses. Top with freshly grated nutmeg and serve immediately.

It was quite dark now, a dreary misty December day – Christmas was only five days ahead. London had been dark and dreary; the country was no less so, though occasionally rendered cheerful with its constant clusters of lights as the train flashed through towns and stations.

4.50 from Paddington, Agatha Christie

Throughout my childhood, a couple of weeks before each Christmas, an eagerly anticipated copy of the local newspaper would be thrown over our fence. In it, all the most extravagantly and/or artistically decorated houses in Brisbane would be listed, and Lucy and I would descend upon it with a highlighter, marking out our route. It was a different time, from an environmental standpoint, and I can't imagine that it still happens in the same way now. But for the month of December, as we sweltered in the evening heat, some incredibly committed Brisbane residents turned a truly baffling number of Christmas lights on, and welcomed strangers into their homes (or at least onto their front lawns) each night.

It's hard to convey the level of spectacle and sparkle if you haven't seen it. Balconies lined with carollers on the busy nights leading up to Christmas. Cars filled with families parking streets away from the big-ticket houses, and trooping on foot in their hundreds to stand and gawk at the sheer luminescent excess. Scheduled nightly visits from Santa – dressed in red board shorts and a tank top, obviously – with a bag of presents slung over his shoulder. A glow from hundreds of thousands of fairy lights making the houses easy to find. Brisbane has a tropical climate, but it didn't stop people covering their lawns in piles of fake snow, sleighs and reindeer.

One year, on the way back from an early Christmas Eve dinner with our dad and stepmother, when the sun had set (but hours before midnight mass), we decided to take the long way home, and loop past some of the houses we had missed earlier in the month. Homeowners were still out on their lawns, whole families welcoming those coming to admire the lights, handing out mince pies and squares of coconut ice.

Australia isn't somewhere I imagine I'll ever live again, but remembering nights like these makes me really miss it. I love my winter Christmases whole-heartedly, and in my eleven years in the UK, I have never yet travelled back for an Australian one. But I think back so fondly to that Christmas Eve night: being among neighbours and friends and strangers, belting out carols, watching people admire the straight lines of lights as they descended the sloped roofs, pointing out little details that had been added since the year before, and listening to hordes of parents gently break it to their small children that it's definitely not something they're going to do at home next Christmas.

Here in England, the lights never fail to thrill me. Like that moment in *4.50 from Paddington*, I spend my frequent train journeys west with my nose glued to the window, keeping an eye out for villages lit up as we pass. A walk up to the Common above Stroud reveals each village in the valleys below twinkling brightly, dressed up for the season, and that first post-sunset visit to Seven Dials in Central London, once the lights have been switched on for the season, is always a joy. But, honestly, they'll always slightly pale in comparison to the extraordinary houses in Chermside, or Banyo, or Upper Mount Gravatt.

'TWAS THE NIGHT BEFORE NIGHT BEFORE CHRISTMAS

The battle opened, as it were, with the Christmas stockings. These, in thickest worsted, bought specially for the occasion, were handed to the guests just before bedtime on Christmas Eve, with instructions that they were to be hung up on their bedposts by means of huge safety pins, which were also distributed.

Christmas Pudding, Nancy Mitford

The Christmas Eves of my teenage years were spent at an annually rotating carousel of family events – with my stepmother's family near the bay, with my mum's dad and my cousins, or with family friends on our street. I have always had an abundance of family (at one point I had seventeen living grandparents and great-grandparents), and so fitting in seeing all the family meant multiple Christmas lunches and dinners in the days surrounding the twenty-fifth. But wherever we were on Christmas Eve, there would be prawns, or fish, or crab, and a buffet of cold salads and soft bread rolls – nothing that required turning the oven on.

Late at night, we'd make our way up the road for midnight mass, where our sweaty legs would stick to the plastic seats as we watched the younger children perform a nativity, and sang carols and hymns with the church choir. I found myself questioning the faith that I had been brought up in pretty early on, and so I was more there for the songs, the prayers having long since become literal lip service. After mass, we'd return home to a slice of toasted panettone spread with brandy butter, and a late-night dip in the pool, before we hung up our Christmas stockings and went to bed. It was always a lovely evening but, in all honesty, a mere precursor to the day itself; I spent most of it happily anticipating Christmas morning.

Since moving to England, my Christmas Eves have been Swedish ones. My Cotswolds family is half Swedish, and so I quickly became familiar with Kalles caviar squeezed from a tube onto boiled eggs, with Jansson's temptation, with shot glasses of aquavit, with meatballs and cream-laced gravy, with gingerbread houses that were destroyed by wooden spoons, and with *sill* (not, as I thought that first year, seal – but pickled herring). Christmas Eve was the big night, with up to fifteen of us squeezed around the table in the kitchen, making our way through increasingly plentiful courses of fish and meat. Though the additional guests sometimes swelled and sometimes shrank, the family was a reliable six of us: Chris and Ingela, Anna and Tom, their cousin Mia and, to my great and grateful joy, me.

If these are traditions and menus unfamiliar to you, and you want some literary inspiration to help you get into the Swedish Christmas spirit, Sven Nordqvist's *Findus* series is a gorgeous place to start. His beautifully illustrated stories all feature Pettson and his cat Findus, enjoying various pastimes – gardening, celebrating birthdays – and there are a couple of lovely ones that see them celebrate Santa Lucia (Findus totters around with a candle crown on his head), and one where they prepare the tree and menu for Christmas Eve, which feels particularly like our Christmas.

It's been a couple of years since we've hosted a proper Swedish Christmas Eve. Ingela, the architect and primary enthusiast of our Christmases, died in 2018. It's perhaps inevitable that grief now colours the lead-up to a day that was once so inextricably hers. The recipes and rituals that she held dear feel strange in her absence. But I still feel most tangibly connected to Ingela when I stand in her kitchen, working my way through recipes I first made with her, imagining her chastising me for failing to put an apron on. Those first years, the whole menu felt overwhelming for a smaller group of us. We each have our favourite parts of the meal, and so we simply made those. Though Christmas Eve won't ever be the same as it was when we shared it with her, having those familiar dishes on the table feels an important part of the season to continue to celebrate.

Stovetop rice pudding

As Findus and Pettson (in Sven Nordqvist's *Findus at Christmas*) worry about all they don't yet have in place for Christmas Eve – no gingerbread, no *lutfisk*, no Christmas tree – they reassure themselves that at least they have the ingredients to make rice pudding for breakfast. I'm happy to copy them in this morning repast. Though usually considered a dessert, rice pudding is not *that* far removed from a rich porridge – a grain, cooked in milk, with a bit of sugar and spice. It feels extraordinarily luxurious eaten while still in pyjamas.

ENOUGH TO FEED THE FIRST TWO OF YOU TO WAKE

30g/2tbsp butter
75g/scant ½ cup pudding rice
150ml/⅔ cup water
A pinch of salt

250ml/1 cup milk
100ml/scant ½ cup double/heavy cream
2tsp caster/superfine sugar
A pinch of ground cinnamon

1. Melt half of the butter in a small saucepan over a low heat. Add the rice, and stir for a minute or two, then add the water and salt. Bring to a gentle simmer, cover, and cook over a low heat for 10 minutes.

2. Pour in the milk, cream and sugar. Stir, cover, reduce the heat to as low as possible, and leave to just barely simmer (without stirring) for 30 minutes until the rice is tender.

3. Once tender, turn off the heat, cover, and leave to sit for 10 minutes before stirring in the remaining butter. Serve with a healthy pinch of cinnamon on top. This should set you up for the day ahead.

Lussekatter (saffron buns)

Traditionally, you would be eating these saffron buns on 13 December for the festival of Santa Lucia. In the old almanac, Lucia Night was the longest of the year. On this day, all across Sweden (and throughout Scandinavia), a Lucia in a long white dress makes her way down the church aisle, her crown made of glowing candles, a trailing procession of handmaidens and star boys with handheld candles in her wake. She is said to bring light and warmth to ward off dark spirits – just right for the darkest day of the year. If there's not a service happening near you, a batch of saffron buns should put you in the spirit – as good mid-morning on Christmas Eve as they are on the thirteenth. They come in a variety of configurations, but I love these swirly s-shapes, like I used to draw when I was young and trying to make my handwriting fancier.

MAKES 12 BUNS, ENOUGH TO TIDE YOU OVER WITH A MID-MORNING COFFEE

85g/6tbsp butter
250ml/1 cup whole milk
⅛tsp saffron threads
225g/scant 1¾cups plain/all-purpose flour
225g/scant 1¾cups strong white bread flour

1tsp fine sea salt
5g/1tsp fast-action yeast
75g/scant ½ cup caster/superfine sugar
2 eggs
24 sultanas/golden raisins

1. Melt the butter in a small saucepan, then add the milk and warm over a low heat until it reaches body temperature. Remove from the heat and add the saffron.

2. Tip the flours into the bowl of a mixer (or a regular mixing bowl if you're making the dough by hand), along with the salt on one side of

the bowl, and the yeast on the other. Pour in the saffron-hued milk. Mix with a dough hook for 5–10 minutes until smooth and elastic (it will take more like 15 minutes if you're working with it by hand). Cover the bowl and leave to rise for an hour, or until doubled in size.

3. While the dough is rising, beat together the sugar and one of the eggs in a bowl. Once the dough has puffed up, and springs back when prodded, add the sugar and egg, kneading until it is all incorporated evenly, and the dough is soft and elastic again.

4. Cut the dough into twelve even pieces. Roll each segment into a 30cm/12in length, and then coil both ends, in opposite directions, like snail shells, until they meet in the middle. Place the S-shaped coils on lined baking sheets (give them some space to swell) and then poke a sultana into the centre of each coil. When you have completed all the coils, cover the sheets and leave to rise for another hour, until they are plump, and bounce back when gently prodded.

5. While the dough is rising, preheat the oven to 220°C/425°F/ Gas 7. Beat the remaining egg and brush the buns with it, then bake for 10–12 minutes, until browned, and hollow sounding when tapped on the bottom.

Gubbröra

This is the perfect thing to pull together in the early afternoon, while everyone is in and out of the kitchen, and dinner is still frustratingly far away. It makes use of ingredients you'll already have to hand, thanks to the Christmas Eve menu (eggs, a tube of caviar, tinned fish, herbs), and is easy to assemble, and to eat. Also, literally translated, it means 'old man's mix', which I find inordinately pleasing.

ENOUGH FOR 4 COOKS TO ENJOY AS A SNACK

4 whole eggs plus 2 egg yolks
1tbsp Kalles caviar (you can find tubes of it online or in IKEA)
1 spring onion/scallion, finely sliced
5 sprigs parsley, chopped
5 sprigs dill, chopped
6 sprat fillets/*ansjovis* (or 3 anchovies, rinsed), roughly diced
Ground white pepper
Rye crispbreads, to serve

1. Bring a small saucepan of water to the boil. Once it has reached a rolling boil, lower in the four eggs, and keep at a simmer for 8½ minutes.

2. Meanwhile, whisk the egg yolks and caviar together in a serving bowl. Mix in the spring onion and herbs, then add the sprats or anchovies, and the white pepper to taste.

3. Run the eggs under cold water until they're cool enough to touch, then peel and dice. Fold into the herb and spring onion mix. Serve heaped onto crispbreads.

Beetroot gravadlax with cucumber pickle and horseradish sauce

This is impossibly festive and beautiful, and will have people raving over your skills long into January. It takes a bit of thought and planning, as you need to start it a couple of days in advance, but planning is par for the course at this time of year – it's not as if Christmas Eve is going to arrive unannounced. The trickiest part is making sure you have space in the fridge, and trying not to slosh beetroot juice all over your kitchen floor as you transfer it in (I, far too clumsy to really be permitted in kitchens, have done this more than once).

MAKES ENOUGH FOR 12

GRAVADLAX
1kg/2¼lb side of salmon, skin-on
3 raw beetroot/beets, scrubbed
6 juniper berries, crushed
Zest of 1 lemon
5 sprigs dill, chopped
100g/½ cup rock salt
50g/¼ cup demerara/turbinado sugar
100ml/scant ½ cup gin

CUCUMBER PICKLE
2 cucumbers

2tbsp rock salt
100ml/scant ½ cup white wine vinegar
2tbsp granulated sugar
1tbsp coriander seeds
Fronds from 5 sprigs of dill

HORSERADISH SAUCE
3tbsp grated horseradish (from a jar, or from the root)
100g/scant ½ cup natural/plain yogurt
Juice of 2 lemons
Black pepper

1. You'll need a decent-sized dish with a lip for this – if your salmon won't fit in whole, slice it in half and place the two pieces side by side. If the fillet is skinless, line the dish with parchment paper. It's important that the salmon lies flat, and skin-side down.

2. Finely chop the beetroot (I'm lazy, and blitz them in a food processor), and add the juniper, lemon zest, dill, salt and sugar. Pour

in the gin. Pack this onto the salmon, ensuring it is entirely covered. Cover with plastic wrap and store in the fridge for between 24 and 48 hours (the longer you leave it, the stronger the cure will be on the salmon).

3. On the day you plan to eat the salmon, prepare the cucumbers. Slice them into long, thin ribbons with a vegetable peeler, and place in a bowl. Sprinkle over the salt and leave for an hour, to leach out some of the water. Bring the vinegar, sugar and coriander seeds to a simmer in a saucepan. Leave the mixture to sit for a couple of minutes to cool slightly, while you squeeze out the cucumber and then rinse it in some cold water. Pour the vinegar over the cucumber. Place in the fridge until chilled, then add the dill fronds.

4. To make the horseradish sauce, mix the horseradish, yogurt and lemon juice together. Season with plenty of pepper.

5. Scrape the cure off the salmon, and then rinse the last of it off with a little splash of cold water. Slice the salmon very thinly, at an angle, starting at the thin tail end, and working your way up. Give yourself time to do this, as it does take a while and you don't want to be stressed or rushed once you have guests. Once sliced, it will keep, covered, in the fridge, for the next couple of days.

6. Serve the sliced salmon with a bowl of the cucumber pickle, the horseradish sauce, and some extra wedges of lemon.

Swedish meatballs

My favourite thing about a Swedish smörgåsbord is that there's no 'centrepiece' on which all your hopes and your reputation must rest. On any other night, these meatballs would be a meal in themselves, but on Christmas Eve they're only part of it – a mere corner of the table we see spread with food in *Findus at Christmas*. They're undeniably great but, really, this is all about the gravy, so do taste it as you go. You want it rich, and savoury, so make sure there's plenty of soy and Worcestershire sauce before adding the cream.

SERVES 6 (OR MORE AS PART OF A SMÖRGÅSBORD)

MEATBALLS
300g/10½oz minced/ground beef
200g/7oz minced/ground pork
60g/1 cup soft white breadcrumbs
1tbsp chopped parsley
1tsp ground allspice
½tsp ground nutmeg
1 brown onion, finely diced
2 cloves garlic, minced
1 egg
Salt and white pepper

50ml/3½tbsp vegetable oil

SAUCE
30g/2tbsp butter
30g/3¾tbsp plain/all-purpose flour
300ml/1¼ cups beef stock
1tbsp Worcestershire sauce
1tsp Dijon mustard
2tsp soy sauce
100ml/scant ½ cup double/heavy cream

1. First, make the meatballs. Put all the ingredients, except the oil, in a large mixing bowl and season with salt and pepper. Squash together using your hands until well combined, and then roll generous teaspoons of the mixture into balls. Pour the oil into a frying pan, and warm over a low heat. Fry the meatballs until golden all over, and cooked through – do break one open to make sure. You can refrigerate or freeze them at this point and reheat when needed.

2. While the meatballs are frying, make a start on the sauce. Melt the butter in a saucepan, and stir the flour into it. Cook for a couple of minutes. Pour the beef stock in slowly, and whisk until it starts to

thicken. Season with the Worcestershire sauce, Dijon mustard, soy sauce, and salt and pepper. Taste to make sure you're happy, then add the cream and remove from the heat.

3. Pour the gravy into the pan with the meatballs and take them to the table like this. Serve as part of a smörgåsbord, or with a scoop of mashed potato and some peas if you want to go full IKEA. Some lingonberry jam is ideal alongside it too.

It was the day before Christmas Eve and barely a crumb was left in the cottage. Today was really the last chance to buy the Christmas food and fell the Christmas tree and bake the gingerbread and fix everything that needed to be fixed for Christmas.

Findus at Christmas, Sven Nordqvist

After the lush, generous, multi-course smörgåsbord that is consumed on Christmas Eve, something sweet is the last thing on anyone's mind. But despite our disinclination towards dessert, we would always have utilized a good chunk of time in the hours preceding dinner to prepare a gingerbread house. There's a pleasing literary history here – though gingerbread had been made in Germany since the sixteenth century, and there are suggestions that it was being made in Greece and France centuries before that, the popularity of building gingerbread houses rose thanks to the Brothers Grimm and their tale of *Hansel and Gretel*.

I have mixed feelings about gingerbread houses. Unlike most food I am passionate about, where it's the eating that I am predominantly focused on, the joy of a gingerbread house is very much in the planning, making and decorating – especially if you buy the parts for the 'house' itself for a couple of quid from IKEA, as we always have. Our thrill was in finding increasingly ridiculous ways to commemorate the year just gone, using only sweets and hard-set caramel.

I vividly remember gluing a picture of Hugh Jackman's face onto a tiny stuffed koala the year we did an Australian house. We made the roof look like corrugated iron, and Kylie and Jason swam in a pool of blue sweets out the back. The Christmas after the Olympics, we made a London 2012 Days of Christmas house: Mo Farah running across the roof, the Opening Ceremony sheep surrounding the house, Anish Kapoor's *Orbit* reimagined in red liquorice in the garden. There was a crime scene house one year too; I think that might have been the winter we were all really into *The Wire*. Regardless of the decoration, after we'd cleared away dinner, the gingerbread house would come out, and we'd attack it viciously with wooden spoons, in order to access the treasure (more sweets, of course) within.

Like many traditions, this one fell by the wayside – the sight of the house, utterly destroyed by our enthusiasm with the wooden spoons, and generally unappealing in taste and texture, was too much waste to continue facing year after year. But then, in 2016, I took a job as a nanny. As Christmas approached, I turned the huge apothecary chest in the kitchen, with its twenty-four deep drawers, into an enormous Advent Calendar: one drawer opened each day until Christmas Eve. In early December, the kids opened a drawer to find my handmade templates; we made a gingerbread house from scratch after school that afternoon, and decorated it that weekend with the sweets I hid in the next day's drawer. This house, with its perfect peaked roof, and dusting of snow, made from slabs of richly spiced homemade gingerbread, was one we all consumed with gusto.

Jansson's temptation

I think this might be my favourite part of the smörgåsbord. It's really just an extravagant potato bake, filled with cream, and salty-sweet sprats, and so of course it's entirely delicious. The leeks here are terribly inauthentic – they should really be diced onion – but my pal Lean (who photographed this book) is sensitive to onion, and so I made this version for her. It was one of those perfect, happy discoveries; we actually preferred it that way. Traditionally, this is eaten on Christmas Eve, but it's worked its way onto my 'Friday night supper' list too – a welcome dish of comfort throughout winter.

SERVES 6–8 (OR MORE AS PART OF A SMÖRGÅSBORD)

60g/¼ cup cold butter

1.2kg/2¾lb Charlotte potatoes (or another waxy variety)

2 medium leeks, washed and finely diced

250g/9oz sprat fillets/*ansjovis**

400ml/1¾ cups whole milk

300ml/1¼ cups double/heavy cream

2tbsp Kalles caviar (optional)

1tbsp tomato purée/paste

A pinch of white pepper

3tbsp dried breadcrumbs

* Try to find tins of cured Swedish sprat fillets, like Grebbestad's, rather than substituting anchovies, which will be far too salty (and I say this as a devoted tinned anchovy lover). They're easy to find online.

1. Preheat the oven to 200°C/400°F/Gas 6 and grease a large baking dish with a tablespoon of the butter. Peel the potatoes and cut into thick matchsticks, about the size of a French fry.

2. Put a third of the potatoes in the base of the dish, then add half the leeks. Arrange half the sprats over the top, retaining the liquid from the tin. Cover with more potatoes, more leeks, more sprats, and then finish with the final third of the potatoes.

3. Pour the milk, cream, liquid from the sprats, caviar (if using), tomato purée and pepper into a jug, and pour over the potatoes. You should just be able to see the liquid through the top layer of potatoes.

4. Slice the rest of the butter into thin slices and lay over the top. Sprinkle with the breadcrumbs, then bake in the centre of the oven for an hour. Allow to cool for 10 minutes before serving.

Endive and walnut salad

Alongside the meatballs (p89) and Jansson's temptation (p96), both rich and full of cream, I always fancy something fresh and crisp and sharp. This is my favourite take on a salad we make (or that Ingela often tasked one of our guests with bringing along). The bitter endive marries well with the sweet pear and salty, sharp Roquefort, but if you want something slightly less rich, you can leave the cheese out.

SERVES 6–8 AS PART OF A SMÖRGÅSBORD

4 heads chicory/endive
2 pears (ripe is ideal, but they're an elusive beast; firm is better than mushy)
100g/3½oz Roquefort
1tsp cider vinegar
1tsp Dijon mustard

1tbsp olive oil
Salt and black pepper
50g/⅓ cup walnuts, toasted and chopped
Small handful of pomegranate seeds
20g/1 cup parsley leaves
20g/½ cup cress

1. Trim the base off the chicory heads and rinse the leaves. Cut the pears into quarters, then core and slice into thin wedges. Toss these together, and crumble the Roquefort over the top.

2. Whisk the vinegar, mustard and oil together, then season with salt and pepper. Toss through the salad, then top with the walnuts, pomegranate seeds, parsley and cress.

Beetroot salad

When preparing a Swedish smörgåsbord, a considerable amount of the work is best described as 'spooning things out of jars'. This means that there's a job for everyone in the kitchen – even the most reluctant cooks. We play music, someone sets the table, a few of us chop and dice and prep, and someone gets jars out of the cupboard: crinkle-cut pickled cucumbers, slices of beetroot, lingonberry jam, various varieties of *sill* (pickled herring) and a Swedish mustard. Depending on how ambitious we're feeling, most of them also come together in this salad – perfect alongside the meatballs (p89), the Jansson's (p96), or with leftover ham (p52) in a sandwich.

SERVES 6–8 AS PART OF A SMÖRGÅSBORD

2tbsp crème fraîche/sour cream
1tbsp mayonnaise
1tsp Swedish mustard
6 whole pickled beetroot/beets
2 crisp eating apples

Juice of ½ lemon
10 Swedish dill pickle slices, finely diced
Sea salt and white pepper
Fronds from 8 sprigs of dill

1. Mix the crème fraîche, mayonnaise and mustard together in whatever serving bowl you're using.

2. Chop the beetroot and unpeeled apples into small dice and place in the serving bowl with the dressing. Squeeze over the lemon juice and toss well to combine.

3. Add the pickles to the bowl, then taste and season with salt and white pepper. Scatter over the dill fronds just before serving.

Pepparkakor

If you visit IKEA in the months leading up to Christmas, there's a good chance you'll end up bringing a huge tin of these home. Mine disappear quickly; I love to have a small stack of biscuits on the go, to be dunked in coffee or eaten alongside a good, rich blue cheese. They're great homemade too, and if Pippi Longstocking (a notoriously chaotic cook) can make hundreds of them, so can you. Though perhaps roll them out on your work surface, rather than (as she does) your floor.

MAKES AT LEAST 60

50ml/3½tbsp water
2tbsp golden syrup/light corn syrup
80g/heaped ⅓ cup light brown sugar
20g/1½tbsp dark brown sugar
1tsp ground ginger

1tsp ground cinnamon
A pinch of ground cloves
75g/⅓ cup unsalted butter, cubed
1tsp bicarbonate of soda/baking soda
220g/1⅔ cups plain/all-purpose flour

1. Bring the water, golden syrup, sugars and spices to the boil over a low heat. Put the butter in a mixing bowl, and pour over the spiced syrup. Leave for a few minutes, until the butter has melted.

2. Sift in the bicarbonate of soda and flour, stir to combine and bring together into a dough. Leave the bowl in the fridge for at least an hour.

3. Preheat the oven to 220°C/425°F/Gas 7. Flour your work surface, and roll out the dough as thinly as you can. Line a couple of baking sheets with parchment paper. Cut hearts or stars out of the dough, or use the rim of a glass to cut circles if you prefer. Arrange them on the sheet, leaving a little space for them to spread slightly. A palette knife or flat knife will help you pick the biscuits up. This dough is incredibly forgiving, so you can roll and re-roll as often as you need.

4. Bake in batches for 5 minutes, until slightly crisp at the edges. Leave to cool a little on the baking sheet, then on a wire/cooling rack.

Meringues and cream

On Christmas night, after a little cold leftover turkey, and just before they head to bed, the Fossil children in Noel Streatfeild's *Ballet Shoes* have meringues and cream. It's what I so often had at Christmas growing up – pavlova – but honestly, dessert for me on Christmas Day is only ever going to be a proper Christmas pudding, and perhaps a slice of Christmas cake later on in the evening. I am suggesting these meringues for Christmas Eve instead then, once your smörgåsbord has settled. Use any fruit you fancy here (you can certainly find something more seasonal than berries) but I love soft red fruits with the light cream and crisp meringue.

SERVES 4

PAVLOVA
3 egg whites
160g/generous ¾ cup caster/superfine sugar (even better if it is vanilla scented – store your sugar with a couple of split vanilla pods/beans for a few weeks beforehand)
1½tsp cornflour/cornstarch
1tsp cream of tartar

TOPPING
300ml/1¼ cups double/heavy cream
Redcurrants, raspberries or other soft fruit
Icing/confectioners' sugar, for dusting

1. Preheat your oven to 180°C/350°F/Gas 4. Draw four 10cm/4in circles on a sheet of greaseproof/wax paper, flip it over, and use it to line a baking sheet.

2. In a spotlessly clean bowl, beat your egg whites to soft peaks. You can do this by hand, but if you have a mixer or electric whisk, now would be the time to employ it. Once at soft peaks, start adding the sugar, a tablespoon at a time. Beat on a high speed for another 3 minutes until the meringue is smooth, glossy and stiff.

3. Take a pinch of the meringue between your fingers and rub it. If you

can still feel the grains of sugar, beat it a bit longer – the undissolved sugar will make your pavlovas weep in the oven. Once the sugar is completely dissolved, sprinkle the cornflour and cream of tartar over the meringue and gently fold it in.

4. Divide the meringue evenly between the four traced circles, and create a slight indent in the middle of each one, where the filling will sit. Transfer the baking sheet to the oven, immediately reduce the temperature to 140°C/275°F/Gas 1 and bake for 50 minutes. When the pavlovas are crisp on top, turn the oven off, leave the door ajar and allow them to cool completely.

5. Whisk the cream for the topping to soft peaks. Serve each pavlova with a dollop of cream, some soft red fruit and a dusting of icing sugar.

… the Vestry door curtains fell back to each side: out came the great Cathedral crosses and blessed banners, with all the Cathedral Choir and Clergy, with all voices lifted aloft in 'Come, all ye Faithful'.

The Box of Delights, John Masefield

My childhood was spent in church choirs, and then school choirs, singing carols and hymns in four- and six-part harmony. I have vivid memories of my favourite performances: the year we sang 'Silent Night' in a cathedral in the centre of Brisbane as a storm raged outside, an unexpectedly moving rendition of 'Joy to the World' that we sang at Midnight Mass the year my grandmother and two step-grandfathers had died. I might have a complicated relationship with the church I grew up in, but my feelings towards its music, especially at Christmas, are wholeheartedly positive.

Like the shifting and changing of Christmas traditions, the canon of Christmas music continues to grow and expand. Early pagans sang as part of the winter solstice celebrations, and it is generally accepted that the first Christmas carol was 'Angels Hymn', first sung in 129AD. Since then, countless songs have been written in honour of Christmas and of winter – 'While Shepherds Watch Their Flocks by Night' in the Middle Ages, 'Coventry Carol' from Medieval England, 'Good King Wenceslas' in the Victorian era. Carols survived Cromwell's banning in the sixteenth century, and in the late nineteenth century the first Christmas carol service was held in Truro in Cornwall.

My early Christmases in England brought with them new carols – the Church of England Midnight Mass is, of course, different from the Catholic Midnight Mass I grew up with. And while 'Hark! The Herald

Angels Sing' and 'Joy to the World' work on both sides of the equator, there's something (I suspect it's the 'bleak midwinter' bit) about 'In the Bleak Midwinter' that means it was never really a runaway hit in Brisbane. Happily, my move here means I can now enjoy it with gusto; it's been my favourite for years.

It would be restrictive, and wrong, though, to keep the focus here entirely on Christmas carols. Christmas music is a wide and hospitable church; though perhaps not quite wide enough, as anyone who ventures into a supermarket or high street shop after mid-November, listening to the same music on a loop, can attest. Personally, I am a sucker for it. I love those first reminders of my favourites each year. Growing up, we'd be woken every morning with Bing Crosby, Joni Mitchell, Dean Martin, or Louis Armstrong; our muggy December days starting with songs about snow and ice-skating. Years later, I am always happy to be greeted with these old favourites halfway down the Waitrose crisps aisle.

These morning songs are a habit that has been hard to shake, even 12,000 miles from home, without my Christmas-loving stepdad, Geoff, stacking up his records and CDs ready for the season. Each year I make a Christmas playlist – Vince Guaraldi Trio, Mariah Carey, *The Muppet Christmas Carol* soundtrack, Sufjan Stevens, the choir of King's College Cambridge, Ella Fitzgerald – plug in my headphones, and take the season with me whenever I venture out into the world.

A BIRD
IN THE
OVEN

'You shall then, after dinner; for of course you know that we all dine early.'

'But blindman's buff at three, with snap-dragon at a quarter to four – charades at five, with wine and sweet cake at half-past six, is ponderous'...

'I ask you to answer me fairly. Is not additional eating an ordinary Englishman's ordinary idea of Christmas-day?'

'I am only an ordinary Englishwoman and therefore cannot say.'

Orley Farm, Anthony Trollope

Throughout childhood, it was pretty much impossible to pretend that my Christmases looked anything like the ones in my favourite books. In place of the roaring fires and drifts of snow that I saw in *Little Women* and *The Children of Greene Knowe*, we had muggy, sweaty days, and looked forward with near desperation to the years we were at my aunt's house because she had air conditioning in her lounge. Rather than the winter walks and snowball fights in *Harry Potter and the Philosopher's Stone*, we played backyard cricket, and took dips in the pool. Instead of the hot roast turkey and Christmas pudding in *Lucy & Tom's Christmas*, we had cold ham, prawns and pavlova.

We did find ways of bringing in the 'classic' culinary Christmas elements in more palatable and seasonally appropriate ways: my dad's ice-cream bombe has crumbled pudding set into brandy-scented ice cream, and we always had potatoes, though ours were boiled and sliced into salads rather than roasted until crisp in goose fat. We watched films where the familiar characters were bundled up against the cold, while a pedestal fan moved soupy air around us. I read *A Christmas Carol* before I went to sleep, having stripped the bed of anything thicker than a sheet.

But, on closer consideration, the similarities between my Christmases and the ones I was reading about were important, tangible ones – it seemed that despite our lack of snow, there was something universal about those things that the season brings. As the Pooters sit down for a 'pleasant' country Christmas in *The Diary of a Nobody*, I thought of our family bickering lovingly, talking over each other as we brought various dishes to the table. Laurie Lee, in his childhood *Village Christmas* reminiscences, recalls 'whiskers of pale flame [that] purr and flicker' around the pudding, just like they did at our house. And the description of the second, evening, Christmas feast in *The Country Child* – a hodgepodge of Christmas cake, potted meats, cold pie and sweet tarts – chimed with my belief that the assembled plates we'd pull together on Christmas night were even more delicious than the lunchtime roast spread.

When I had my first Christmas Day in England, I experienced an intense impulse to make up for lost time – to have the 'proper' English Christmas I'd always dreamed of: wintry scenes, roast turkey, mulled wine, a roaring fire. I often find, whether I'm aware of it or not, that my childhood self creeps in, supplying ideas and pictures of how things should look, and taste, and be. I have relished, of course, being able to embrace the rituals I'd wanted to enjoy for so long. But I think I also occasionally lost sight of what it is I had always loved most about Christmas Day when I was growing up.

As I've grown older, inevitably, there are years where things happen differently, where life waltzes in and forces a change. Having so carefully built these rituals, I have a tendency to become anxious when they alter. However, regardless of where I spend Christmas: with my family in the Cotswolds; with friends in London; in a Shelter women's refuge, catering with my best friend Liv, I can bring the parts of it I most value with me. All those universal elements of the season that I loved about my years in Australia are ones that I have managed to find in England too, in so many different places. And so, wherever I spend it, I relish the chance to consider exactly what I wish to bring (quite literally) to the table. The recipes that follow will, I trust, work on your Christmas table as well as they do on mine.

Buckwheat blinis for breakfast

The March sisters' breakfast, the one they end up giving away, is a memorable spread. I grew up watching the 1994 film, and I can still see Winona Ryder reach for a sausage before they're sitting around the table, and Kirsten Dunst with an orange tucked under her chin. But it's the buckwheats, little Civil War-era pancakes, that I fancy for my Christmas breakfast. The March girls didn't have salmon, but I see no reason for us to recreate their breakfast *too* faithfully, especially if you have any gravadlax leftover from yesterday.

ENOUGH FOR 8

BLINIS
60g/⅓ cup buckwheat flour
60g/⅓ cup strong white bread flour
A pinch of salt
A pinch of sugar
100ml/scant ½ cup milk
10g/2tsp fresh yeast (or 3g/1tsp fast-
action yeast)*
75g/5tbsp sour cream
1 egg yolk

2 egg whites
30g/2tbsp butter

TO SERVE
Smoked salmon, or leftover gravadlax
from yesterday (p87)
100g/3½tbsp sour cream
Dill sprigs
Juice of 1 lemon

* I like the flavour of fresh yeast here, but if you can't get hold of it, easy/fast-action is great too.

1. Whisk together the flours, salt and sugar in a mixing bowl. Warm the milk to body temperature in a saucepan, then stir in the yeast until it dissolves. Whisk in the sour cream, and the egg yolk.

2. Pour the liquid ingredients into the flour and whisk thoroughly. Cover the bowl with a tea towel and put it in a draught-free place to rise for an hour (it might take a little longer than this on Christmas morning, so feel free to get your bird prepped, or stuffing made). The batter should almost double in size.

3. After an hour, beat the egg whites to stiff peaks, and then fold them into the frothy mixture. Cover with the tea towel again and leave for another hour. The mixture should be very light and full of bubbles – almost like a foam.

4. Once the batter has risen, warm half a tablespoon of the butter in a frying pan. Without stirring the mixture (you want to retain the lightness), drop teaspoons of the batter into the pan. When the top of a blini is covered with bubbles, flip it over. Cook the blinis in batches until all the batter is used up, adding more butter when needed.

5. Serve each blini warm, with a twist of salmon, a dollop of sour cream, a sprig of dill, and a squeeze of lemon. They can be warmed through in the oven, but are best fresh, if you can serve them straight away.

Christmas Dinner

On Christmas Day, Scrooge sends a young boy to buy an enormous turkey for the Cratchits. I am sure he meant well, but a guest with an uncooked turkey arriving without warning on Christmas morning might be, at best, a slightly unwelcome sight, especially if your plan had been a roasted goose (a bird I definitely prefer). If I were Mrs Cratchit, I'd find a corner to deposit Scrooge's turkey in, and serve the goose as planned – with apple sauce, mash, stuffing and gravy.

SERVES 8

GOOSE
4–5kg/9–11lb goose
Salt and black pepper

MASH
2kg/4½lb potatoes, peeled and diced
60ml/¼cup whole milk

50g/3½tbsp butter

APPLE SAUCE
50g/3½tbsp butter
1kg/2¼lb Bramley/cooking apples, peeled and diced
3tbsp light brown sugar

1. An hour before your bird needs to go in the oven, remove it from the fridge, take off any packaging, and bring it to room temperature. Preheat the oven to 200°C/400°F/Gas 6.

2. Dry the skin of the goose with kitchen paper. Prick the skin, but not the flesh, with a sharp knife, then rub with salt and pepper. Set up a roasting tray with a rack at the base, so that the fat has somewhere to drain away from the bird. Place the bird on the rack, breast side up and legs as wide apart as possible. Roast for 30 minutes per kg/65 minutes per lb, plus an additional 30 minutes (my 4.3kg/9½lb one took just over two and a half hours).

3. After an hour, remove the goose from the oven and tip the fat from the tray into a bowl. Set this aside for the stuffing (p121), and return the bird to the oven.

4. For the apple sauce: melt the butter in a saucepan, add the diced apples and the sugar, and cook for 15 minutes over a medium heat. Stir occasionally to prevent them browning.

5. Remove the goose from the oven, transfer to a serving dish and cover with a sheet of foil. Leave to rest for 30 minutes while you finish the gravy and make the mash.

6. To make the mash, boil the potatoes until tender. Drain, then mash until smooth. Add the milk and butter and stir through, then season.

7. Carve the goose at the table, and serve it alongside the mash, warm apple sauce, gravy and piping hot stuffing.

Start-in-advance gravy

If you want to make your life easier on Christmas Day, take a leaf out of Mrs Cratchit's book and have the gravy 'ready beforehand in a little saucepan'. There are other things you can do in advance – prepare desserts, parboil potatoes, make the stuffing – but knowing that the gravy is part-way done will take a huge load off. The method is the same whatever bird you're roasting, though you won't have to remove quite so much fat from the pan with a turkey or capon as you do with a goose.

SERVES 8

50g/3½tbsp butter
Goose giblets (not the liver) and wing tips
400g/14oz chicken wings, chopped or broken up
2 onions, roughly chopped
1 carrot, roughly chopped
2 celery sticks, roughly chopped

6 peppercorns
250ml/1 cup white wine
30g/3¾tbsp plain/all-purpose flour
1tsp English mustard
1tsp redcurrant jelly, or to taste
Sea salt and black pepper

1. Melt the butter in a large saucepan over a moderate heat. Fry the giblets, wing tips and chicken wings until browned. Add the roughly chopped vegetables and the peppercorns and cook for a further 10 minutes until softened. Add the white wine, and allow it to bubble away for a couple of minutes.

2. Add 2 litres of water to the pan. Simmer over a low heat for 2 hours to reduce. Strain the stock into a container, leave to cool completely, and store in the fridge for up to 3 days.

3. On Christmas Day, once you take the goose from the oven and set it aside to rest, pour the majority of the fat from the pan (you can use it for the stuffing, or for roasting potatoes). Don't scrape the pan, but don't leave more than a couple of tablespoons of fat behind.

4. Place the roasting pan, with scraps of meat and charred bits, over a low heat and sprinkle in the flour. Stir around until it has cooked for a couple of minutes. Pour a splash of the gravy stock into the pan to loosen everything.

5. Transfer this to a saucepan (fastidiously scraping all the good crispy bits out of the pan). Pour 600ml/2½ cups of the gravy stock into the saucepan, and reduce until it is the consistency you like. Taste it frequently as it simmers away and add the English mustard, as well as a spoonful of redcurrant jelly if it needs sweetening. Season with salt and pepper. Strain the gravy into a serving jug.

Stuffing

Last year, as we peeled potatoes, we all listed our top three Christmas dinner dishes. Everyone advocated for their favourite bits – the bread sauce, the gravy, the potatoes, the sprouts. But the dish that cropped up more than anything else? Stuffing. This is the version we make in our house, cooked in a baking dish rather than in the goose itself. Although we miss the 'long expected gush of stuffing' as the knife is plunged into the Cratchits' bird, we do get a lovely crisp top (and a true abundance of stuffing). There's very little not to love here: bacon *and* chipolatas, fresh herbs, breadcrumbs, goose fat. This works perfectly with the goose and apple sauce on p117; if you're making it alongside a different bird, do swap the goose fat for olive oil.

SERVES 8

3 brown onions, diced
75g/2¾oz goose fat
200g/7oz streaky bacon, sliced
200g/7oz chipolatas, cut into 1cm/½in
  pieces

10g/⅓oz sage, finely chopped
30g/1oz parsley, finely chopped
150g/5½oz soft white breadcrumbs
Sea salt and ground black pepper

1. Preheat the oven to 200°C/400°F/Gas 6. Fry the diced onion in a tablespoon of the goose fat until translucent, then tip into a bowl. Fry the bacon and chipolatas, and add these to the bowl. Add the chopped herbs, along with the breadcrumbs, a pinch of salt, and a very generous grinding of pepper.

2. Warm the remaining goose fat in a saucepan until liquid and pour over the stuffing. Stir through, then transfer to a greased baking dish and bake for 30 minutes.

Grief wellington

As a family, we started to eat less meat a few years ago. It wasn't done with any fanfare; we just started thinking about alternatives instead of defaulting to meat for big occasions. And so, after years of turkeys, capons, beef and ham, one Christmas, we made what Anna affectionately christened a 'grief wellington': a beef wellington, without the beef. Though the filling has altered since that first year, the name stuck.

Serves 8

4 medium carrots (a mix of colours is lovely), peeled and diced into 1cm/½in cubes

1 large or 2 small parsnips, peeled and diced into 1cm/½in cubes

½ celeriac, peeled and diced into 1cm/½in cubes

Leaves from 10 sprigs of thyme

Leaves from 5 sprigs of rosemary

3tbsp olive oil

Sea salt and black pepper

2 brown onions, diced

4 cloves garlic, crushed

½tsp nutmeg

30g/¼ cup hazelnuts, roughly chopped

40g/½ cup grated Parmesan (optional)

Small bunch sage, finely chopped

100g/2 cups soft white breadcrumbs

8 Savoy cabbage leaves

500g/1lb 2oz puff pastry block

1 egg, beaten

1. Preheat the oven to 200°C/400°F/Gas 6. Put the diced carrots, parsnip and celeriac into a roasting pan, add the thyme and rosemary leaves, and toss together with 2 tablespoons of the oil and a generous amount of seasoning. Roast for 25–30 minutes, until the vegetables are tender.

2. Meanwhile, add the remaining tablespoon of oil to a medium saucepan over a moderate heat. Once warm, tip in the diced onions and cook for 10 minutes until softened. Add the garlic and nutmeg and cook for a further 5 minutes. Turn off the heat, and stir in the chopped hazelnuts, Parmesan, sage and breadcrumbs. Add the

roasted vegetables, then tip everything into a bowl and chill in the fridge until completely cold.

3. Cut the woody core out of the cabbage leaves, but keep them whole. Bring a large saucepan of water to the boil and blanch the leaves for a minute, before draining, squeezing, and patting them dry. Lay out a couple of sheets of plastic wrap, and arrange the cabbage leaves into a rough 40 x 30cm/16 x 12in rectangle on top. Lay the chilled filling in a long, heaped line down the middle of the cabbage leaves, then wrap them around it, sealing with the plastic wrap. Pull it tight as you wrap it; you'll end up with a long cabbage-wrapped log. Chill it in the freezer for at least 10 minutes, and then get to work on the pastry.

4. Dust your work surface with flour, and roll the pastry out into a 50 x 30cm/20 x 12in rectangle. Place the filling log in the middle of the pastry, the messy join of the cabbage facing up. Fold the short ends of the pastry over the filling, and then fold one of the long ends over the top. Paint it with a little beaten egg, and then fold the other long end over the top. Pinch it closed.

5. Flip the sealed wellington over and placed on a lined baking sheet. Paint the whole thing with egg wash, and bake for 40 minutes, until golden brown on top, and cooked underneath. Allow to cool for 5–10 minutes before serving in generous slices.

Crisp Brussels sprouts

In *The Green Road*, the sprouts burn on Christmas Day, and Rosaleen reassures everyone that it doesn't really matter, as no one likes them anyway. For me, that couldn't be less true – they're one of my favourite things on the Christmas table. In terms of cooking, I have to say, better a little burnt than over-boiled. Sprouts contain high levels of sulforaphane, which will make them taste like rotten eggs when cooked for too long. Avoid boiling them at all, if you can – young, tender sprouts cooked in a pan to a light char, like they are here, will be sweet and nutty and delicious. You want them 'green as if they had just come from the garden', as they are in *The Country Child*.

SERVES 8

800g/1¾lb Brussels sprouts	1tbsp rice vinegar
2tbsp sesame oil	1tbsp sesame seeds
2tbsp soy sauce	Handful of parsley leaves
1tbsp fish sauce	1 red chilli, deseeded and finely sliced

1. Clean the Brussels sprouts, pull off any grim outer leaves, and trim the stem. Slice in half through the base. Warm a large frying pan over a moderate heat. Pour in the sesame oil and, once hot, add the sprouts. Cook for 6–8 minutes (depending on their size) until the sprouts are tender on the inside, and crisp and charred in places on the outside.

2. Meanwhile, mix the soy sauce, fish sauce and vinegar together in a bowl. Take the sprouts off the heat, add the dressing and toss. Top with the sesame seeds, parsley and chilli and serve immediately.

Merry Christmas, Marilla! Merry Christmas, Matthew! Isn't it a lovely Christmas? I'm so glad it's white. Any other kind of Christmas doesn't seem real, does it? I don't like green Christmases.

Anne of Green Gables, L. M. Montgomery

I did not properly see snow until I was twenty-two. I saw a patch of it beside the road once, aged nineteen, driving through France in winter, and we pulled over so I could thrust my hands into it. It was, unsurprisingly I guess, cold and wet and a bit underwhelming. I made it into a slushy snowball anyway, one that fell apart the minute I attempted to throw it.

A few years later, during my first English winter, I was interning in a freezing pub theatre in Islington, trying to hover as close as possible to the electric heater, as the cold crept in through the floorboards, when it began to snow outside. I had to double check with my colleagues what it was and then squealed, before running outside to stare up at the sky; a moment you will perhaps be familiar with if you have worked with an Australian or a snow novice during the winter months.

I naively expected it to be fluffy and light and pristine white, like I imagined it was in Narnia, at Hogwarts, where the March sisters lived in Concord, as it is always drawn in Shirley Hughes' Christmas books, or when the Jolly Postman cycles through it with his letters and parcels. It is an easy thing to romanticize, of course, to imagine stomping through it, warm and dry in your fur coat and sturdy boots with the Pevensies, throwing perfectly formed snowballs at the Weasley twins, cosy around the tree with Lucy and Tom as the snow falls outside.

In London, snow is rarely like this. It's slushy and wet and grey far too quickly. When it's falling, it clings to your eyelashes, obscuring your vision. It melts its way through layers of clothing. It is messy, and cold, and wonderful. Eleven years on, and I am still as excited to see it as I first was.

To qualify as a White Christmas, technically, snow must fall from the sky on Christmas Day. And so, while I have had a Christmas in the snow, one cold season that we spent sledding down the hills and crunching through drifts of white beneath crystal clear blue skies, a White Christmas still eludes me. And it may continue to do so – last Christmas was alarmingly mild. The mercury read nine degrees at lunchtime, too warm for our afternoon fire, and far too warm for any snow. The world and the climate are changing, degree by terrible degree and, in the south of England at least, the White Christmases in Gloucestershire of days gone by, that Laurie Lee writes of so beautifully, may be behind us. It's a terrifying thought but I live, as ever, in eternal hope.

Roasted figs for a cheeseboard

If there's a lower-fuss and more genuinely fitting end to a meal than a cheeseboard, I have yet to see it. And, on Christmas night, when lingering is the key, it is particularly pleasing – I want something that I can keep returning to as we pop on another film, or commit to a lengthy game of Trivial Pursuit. A cracker, a wedge of some pungent cheese, a smear of chutney, and a little piece of fruit are more than welcome.

In terms of the cheeses themselves, there aren't really any rules – pick ones you like the taste of and build the rest of the board around that. Go to a good cheesemonger, if you have access to one, not least because they might let you taste (which is really half the fun). A good rule of thumb is to go for larger pieces of fewer cheeses – they keep better, and your board will be less overwhelming. Between three and five cheese should work, depending on how many of you there are: one or two hard cheeses (Cheddar, Lincolnshire poacher, Comté, or Lancashire); one or two soft cheeses (Camembert, brie, Époisses); a blue cheese (Stilton is the classic Christmas choice, and the potted one on p14 is lovely, but do give a Stichelton or an Irish Cashel Blue a try); and perhaps a sheep's or goat's cheese (I like an ash-covered goat's cheese, like Dorstone) will serve you well.

Alongside the cheeses – which should always remain the stars of the show – offer some crackers and/or bread, some chutney (the apple, pear and chilli one on p17 is great), and some fruit. Grapes or apple slices are traditional, and work really well, but for special occasions I have started doing some Irish-inspired roasted figs, the 'companion dish… of Smyrna figs' from Joyce's 'The Dead' – a New Year's story, not a Christmas one, but good inspiration nonetheless. They function here as both a fruit and a chutney.

2 Irish breakfast teabags (or any strong
  tea you have in your cupboard)
30g/2tbsp butter
1tbsp honey

1tbsp Irish whiskey
12 fresh figs
40g/3¼tbsp demerara/turbinado sugar

1. Steep the teabags in 2 tablespoons of boiling water for 4 minutes. Melt the butter and honey in a small saucepan. Add the water from the soaked tea bags, and the whiskey. Allow to bubble on the hob for a moment, and then set aside.

2. Slice the figs through the tip almost down to the base, but leave both halves attached. Make another slice to create a cross. Pinch each fig at the base to open it up. Sit them in a baking dish; the tighter they are packed the better, so there's less space for the honey to burn.

3. Preheat the oven to 180°C/350°F/Gas 4. Spoon a little of the honey mixture over each fig, and add a generous sprinkle of demerara sugar. Transfer to the oven for 15 minutes. Serve the figs warm, in a dish alongside the cheeseboard.

Christmas pudding

As he heads up to bed on Christmas night, Paddington Bear takes a generous slice of pudding with him – he's worried he might get hungry and he doesn't want 'to take any chances'. Despite our extensive Christmas Day menu, I know how he feels; I'm always reassured by the thought that I can pop back to the fridge for a slice late at night (warmed in a pan with brandy butter). This recipe is my great-grandmother's; she made them annually for all our family. In Queensland, it was far too hot for pudding, really, but that never stopped us. I've never had a Christmas without one of these.

MAKES 2 PUDDINGS (ONE FOR YOUR FAMILY, ONE TO GIVE AWAY) – EACH PUDDING SERVES 8

1kg/2¼lb mixed dried fruit
1 apple, grated
1 carrot, grated
1tsp grated nutmeg
1tsp ground cinnamon
4tsp mixed spice
1tbsp marmalade
1tbsp golden syrup
75g/1 cup flaked/slivered almonds
125ml/½ cup Bundaberg rum (another golden rum can be substituted, or brandy, if you prefer)
250g/1 cup + 2tbsp butter

220g/1 cup + 2tbsp light brown sugar
4 eggs
130g/1 cup self-raising flour
130g/1 cup plain/all-purpose flour
115g/1½ cups dried breadcrumbs
½tsp salt
50ml/3½tbsp brandy (if you want a flaming pudding)

EQUIPMENT
2 squares of calico/unbleached cotton – 50cm/20in squared
String

1. Soak the dried fruit, apple, carrot, spices, marmalade, syrup and almonds in the rum overnight.

2. Soak the calico in water. Cream the butter and sugar in a large mixing bowl. Add the eggs, one at a time, beating well after each addition. Sift the flours together and fold into the batter, along with the breadcrumbs and salt. Stir in the soaked fruit and rum.

3. Wring out the calico and sprinkle lightly with flour. Divide the mixture into two and spoon each half onto a sheet of calico. Pull up the corners and the edges. Tie with string, leaving a very small hole in the top. This step is easier with two people, as you need to hold around the top of the pudding while pulling the fabric firmly to make a pleasingly rounded pudding. Fill the hole left at the middle of the tie with flour. Knot the corners together to aid lifting out of the water (a wooden spoon provides a good handle here).

4. Bring a large saucepan of water to the boil. Ease the puddings into the pan and bring back to the boil. Reduce the heat and simmer for 7 hours, topping up the water when you need to. Hang the puddings over a bowl to drain overnight. Do not allow them to rest on their bottoms, as this will affect their shape as they dry.

5. Once they have dripped dry, hang the puddings in an airy place to dry out completely. When they are bone dry, including in the folds of the fabric, store in a cool, dark place until Christmas.

6. On Christmas Day, boil the pudding in the calico for an hour. Unwrap and place on a plate. If you want a flaming pudding, gently warm the brandy in a small saucepan. Remove from the heat and, being very careful not to burn yourself, hold a lighted match to the brandy. It should ignite with a blue flame. Pour over the pudding. Serve with custard, rum butter, ice cream or thick cream.

Christmas cake

Regardless of how busy I am in the lead-up to Christmas, I will find time to make a Christmas cake. It does demand some care, especially if you want to make the marzipan and the icing yourself as I do. But it will remain delicious for a good length of time, so you can really draw out your enjoyment. You don't need to make the cake weeks in advance as some do, but I'd recommend leaving yourself a little more time than Gwen does in Susan Cooper's *The Dark is Rising* – she ices her cake on Christmas Eve.

PROVIDES (AT LEAST) 20 SLICES

CAKE
400g/3 cups plain/all-purpose flour
250g/1⅔ cups sultanas/golden raisins
175g/1¼ cups chopped dried dates
125g/1 cup chopped dried apricots
200g/1½ cups chopped prunes
50g/½ cup chopped dried cherries
2tsp ground ginger
A pinch of salt
½tsp bicarbonate of soda/baking soda
200ml/scant 1 cup double/heavy cream
100g/5tbsp treacle/molasses
180g/scant 1 cup light brown sugar
200g/¾ cup + 2tbsp unsalted butter,
  melted and cooled

2 eggs
150g/½ cup apricot jam/jelly

MARZIPAN
100g/½ cup golden caster/superfine
  sugar
150g/1 cup icing/confectioners' sugar,
  plus extra for dusting
250g/2½ cups ground almonds
1 egg (and an extra white, if you need it)

ICING/FROSTING
2 egg whites
500g/3½ cups golden icing/
  confectioners' sugar
Juice of 1 lemon

1. Preheat the oven to 150°C/300°F/Gas 2 and grease and line a 20cm/8in cake pan. Put the flour, dried fruit, ginger, salt and bicarbonate of soda in a mixing bowl and stir to combine. Add the cream, treacle and sugar to the melted butter, and whisk well. Add the wet ingredients to the dry flour mixture and stir through.

2. Whisk the eggs until light and frothy and then fold through the

batter. The mix should be dark, rich and heavy. Spoon into the cake pan and bake for 90 minutes, checking the top after an hour. If it is browning too quickly (mine often do), cover with a sheet of foil. When a skewer inserted into the cake comes out clean, remove it from the oven. Cool on a wire/cooling rack in the pan for 10 minutes, then remove from the pan and leave to cool completely.

3. To make the marzipan*, sift the sugars into a bowl, and add the ground almonds. Mix together with your hands, then add the egg. Again, mix and squelch the marzipan together with your hands: you need to feel when it is ready. The marzipan should come together into a ball, without sticking too much to the bowl or your hands. If it is too dry, add a little egg white. If it is too sticky, add a little more icing sugar. Shape into a ball, wrap in plastic wrap and store in the fridge for at least an hour.

4. When the cake is stone cold (if it is even slightly warm, the marzipan won't stick well to it), you can prepare it for icing. If your cake has domed on top, start by trimming the top so it is flat. Keep the trimmings as sustenance to nibble on; cake decorating is hard work. Flip the cake over and put it bottom-side up on a serving plate.

5. Warm the apricot jam in a small saucepan, then strain it to eliminate any lumps. Brush it over the top and sides of the cake. Dust your work surface with a little icing sugar and roll the marzipan into a circle wide enough to cover your cake (measure this by running a piece of string from the base on one side, over the top and down the other side). As you roll, keep lifting the marzipan up and re-dusting your work surface with icing sugar. If it's warm in your house, you can roll the marzipan between two pieces of greaseproof/wax paper, if you prefer. When your marzipan is large enough, lift it up (using your rolling pin for support, if needed) and lay it over the cake. Smooth

it over the top and down the sides. Trim the excess at the base of the cake, and leave to dry out for a day.

6. To make the icing*, beat the egg whites with an electric whisk until they are frothy. Add two-thirds of the icing sugar, a tablespoon at a time, beating on a high speed until stiff peaks form. Add the last of the icing sugar, along with the lemon juice, and beat until very stiff. Spoon the icing onto the cake, and smooth it over the top, and then around the sides, using a palette knife. If you're worried about getting a smooth finish, little snowy peaks look lovely too. Allow the cake to dry for a day before you cut into it. This icing will also protect it for a few weeks (or longer) if you want to get ahead of yourself; just store it in an airtight box until Christmas.

* If you prefer, your Christmas cake can be covered with marzipan and royal icing from a packet, though you will still need to allow a day or two for each layer to dry properly. But if you want to go the whole hog, it is lovely to make your own.

Smoking bishop

On Christmas night, after his life-changing apparitions have faded, Ebenezer Scrooge shares a smoking bishop with Bob Cratchit. This Victorian version of mulled wine is perfect for a cold evening, and for late-night conversation. If, like me, you adore mulled wine – even the aggressively average stuff that gets passed around at events throughout December – then this will please you no end.

SERVES 2 – GENEROUSLY

10 cloves
1 orange
1 stick of cinnamon
3cm/1¼in piece of fresh ginger
½tsp ground mace
1tsp ground allspice (or 5 crushed
 allspice berries)
325ml/1⅓ cups red wine

175ml/scant ¾ cup Port
2tsp granulated sugar
2 clementines, peeled
Fresh nutmeg, to serve

EQUIPMENT
A small piece of muslin/cheesecloth

1. Preheat the oven to 190°C/375°F/Gas 5. Stick 6 of the cloves into the orange and place it in the oven for around 30 minutes, or until it is lightly browned and filling your kitchen with a strong scent of Christmas.

2. Place the remaining cloves along with the other spices in a small saucepan with 285ml/1¼ cups of water. Bring to the boil and allow to reduce by about half. Turn off the heat and leave to steep for 10 minutes, then strain into a jar. Tie a muslin square over the top of the jar to act as a very fine strainer.

3. Pour the wine and Port into a saucepan and place over a low heat. Once hot, light a match and, very carefully, place it on top of the liquid. The wine should ignite with a blue flame. Allow it to burn for a few seconds and then blow it out. Pour the spiced water into the wine,

and add the orange from the oven. Keep over a low heat for around 10 minutes.

4. To serve, place the sugar in a bowl and roll one of the clementines in it. Squash it around until the sugar turns a light shade of orange, then divide the sugar between two glasses. Squeeze the juice from the clementine and divide it between the glasses as well. Cut the second clementine into thick slices and place one in each glass. Ladle the hot wine into the glasses, stir, then grate a little nutmeg over the top. Serve while still piping hot.

... I staid not, but calling my boy from my Lord's lodgings, and giving Sarah some good advice by my Lord's order, to be sober and look after the house, I walked home again with great pleasure, and there dined by my wife's bedside with great content, having a mess of brave plum-porridge and a roasted pullet for dinner, and I sent for a mince-pie abroad, my wife not being well to make any herself yet.

Samuel Pepys

I'm not sure what your Christmas night looks like, but I spend most of mine in a corner of the sofa. More often than not, I am involved with the cooking and so, once we have retired from the table, I am rarely responsible for the communal tasks to come: washing up, the cheeseboard, a round of teas or whiskies as the evening progresses. It's quite a trick, really – get your jobs out of the way early, and then behave like a queen for the rest of the evening.

In Kate Atkinson's *Behind the Scenes at the Museum*, the sisters spend a Christmas on the sofa, gorging themselves on mince pies and watching television. They're there for tragic reasons – an event has utterly rocked their family – but I still read this scene with a tiny twinge of jealousy. Growing up, thanks to my divorced and remarried parents, an abundance of grandparents, and a vast gaggle of cousins, our Christmas Days were filled with multiple events, and long drives from one dinner to another as we tried to fit everyone in. The result was a distinct lack of downtime; we could just about squeeze in a round of charades, or the forehead/Rizla game, but an hour or two of telly was unimaginable.

One year in England, I had a number of friends at a loose end and organized an orphan's Christmas of sorts: midnight mass in Shoreditch, a sleepover at mine, Christmas lunch and an afternoon walk in an eerily quiet London Fields. My friends made their way back home in the late afternoon, and I, like Pepys, 'walked home again with great pleasure', for an evening nestled into the sofa with a bowl of trifle, and a long list of television episodes to get lost in.

I love storytelling of all forms and so, entirely unsurprisingly, I am a huge fan of television. We're in a golden age of it now, but there's always been something magical about a story that is told in your living room, about opening your home to characters you get to know better and better over the course of years, and of sharing that experience with the other people on your sofa. It's even better at Christmas (for this fan of warmth and sincerity at least) when notoriously prickly characters are softened by tinsel, crackers and silly hats.

I'm here for all of it: Werner Hogg's terrible Christmas party unfolding at *The Office* (and seeing Dawn turn her taxi around to let Tim know how she feels), *Gilmore Girls'* Lorelai, Rory and Emily gathering in a hospital waiting room when Richard suffers a heart attack, *The Vicar of Dibley*'s four Christmas lunch invitions, *The West Wing* staff giving each other gifts while Toby organizes a military funeral, the Doctor (Who, of course) saving the Earth yet again, the Roses decorating Room 6 in the Rosebud Motel in order to give Johnny a *Schitt's Creek* Christmas to remember, the annual Nativity organised by the midwives from Nonnatus House, *Mad Men*'s Don and Joan drinking in a midtown bar, the *Parks and Recreation* team making an edible office for Leslie Knope, Bart shoplifting a video game and then trying make amends with the rest of *The Simpsons*. Even years after they were first broadcast, the very best episodes of Christmas television are worth returning to, year after year.

STARTING
ANEW

'Ah, I see it will not do to preach on New Year's Day,' said Mr. Farebrother, rising and walking away. He had discovered of late that Fred had become jealous of him, and also that he himself was not losing his preference for Mary above all other women.

Middlemarch, George Eliot

I recognize that it is entirely possible that you might be a party-adoring New Year's Eve fan, in which case the next couple of paragraphs will feel unfamiliar to you. But, of all the days in the festive calendar, New Year's Eve is my least favourite. As a teenager, I actively dreaded it. Perhaps it's the years of thwarted romantic expectation, the *When Harry Met Sally* of it all – too many films that suggest that the most important kiss you might have all year will happen at midnight on December thirty-first. Perhaps it's the build up, the dream that this year's party will be better and more fun and wilder than last year. Perhaps it's the inevitable crash at 2 a.m., when you're suddenly desperate to be tucked up in bed, and painfully aware that the journey home is going to be a nightmare. Regardless, whatever the reason, New Year's Eve as a teenager, and as a twentysomething, was a resounding disappointment.

As such, I tend to approach scenes of New Year's Eve parties in literature with a sort of voyeuristic delight, genuinely and properly thrilled not to be there in person. I'm so pleased not to be waking up in the aftermath of a raging house party where Archie and Clara meet on the morning of 1 January in Zadie Smith's *White Teeth*. I don't want to attend the fancy dinner party where *About a Boy*'s Will is among smug strangers, even if it does mean he gets to meet (though also immediately lie to) Rachel. I am a contented fly on the wall as *A Doll's House*'s Torvald and Nora arrive home, still dressed in their party best, and come to an inevitable and shattering conclusion about their marriage.

Adulthood brought with it the happy realization that if I didn't fancy attending a party, literally no one was forcing me to do so. I love that I have friends in my life who aren't particularly interested in big parties, and who want to come round for a very relaxed meal; who welcome whatever it is I want to cook, dinner coming later than usual as we wait for the countdown to midnight. But I also discovered that a night spent with a takeaway and a screening of Jurassic Park before retiring to bed just after twelve was an entirely appropriate way to ring in the New Year. Once I let go of that expectation of what the evening *should* look like, I started to enjoy it for what it was – a night worth marking in a way that makes sense to me.

If you're anything like I am, and feeling somewhat sociable this year, what you will most long for as the next year arrives is the company of a few dear pals, a couple of bottles of something delicious, and some good food to bring to the table. The recipes that follow here aren't fussy, but will make for a beautiful feast – something you can put together with relative ease, and very little that needs much of your active attention. There's a New Year's Eve menu in *The Little Library Year* from *Babette's Feast*: blinis and caviar, individual bird pies, and a gorgeous, impressive cake. I'm not going to lie – it's a joy to eat, but it is undeniably ambitious. Here, I've kept things a fair bit simpler, with a nod to Joyce's 'The Dead', my favourite New Year's story, but mostly with you in mind – encouraging you to have a glass of something in your hand, chatting with your guests, rather than spending the evening in the kitchen.

Pytt i panna

Pytt i panna (literally 'small pieces in a pan') is a sort of Swedish bubble and squeak. Though it can be made from scratch, it usually relies on leftovers: meatballs (p89), boiled potatoes, frankfurters, and chunks of Christmas ham (p52). Use whatever you have around; the only non-negotiables, in my mind, are the beetroot, potato and egg. It's a great breakfast for 31 December; allowing you to greet the new year with slightly fewer boxes of leftovers crowding the fridge.

SERVES 4

125g/4½oz leftover Christmas ham (or pancetta), diced

2 brown onions, diced

600g/1lb 5oz cold cooked potatoes, diced

200g/7oz frankfurter sausages, diced

250g/9oz leftover cooked meatballs, diced

4 whole pickled beetroot/beets, diced

4 hard-boiled eggs, cut into wedges, or 12 quail's eggs, cut in half

A note: The recipe below assumes that you have some leftovers. If you don't: boil potatoes until tender in salted water for about 15 minutes. Lower the quail eggs into simmering water for 3 minutes, or hen eggs for 7 minutes, and then run under cold water. And do cook the meat for a little longer, to ensure it is cooked through.

1. If using pancetta, fry it in a heavy-based pan over a low heat. Once golden, remove from the pan, leaving the fat behind.

2. In the pancetta fat (or 1tbsp groundnut or vegetable oil, if you are using leftover ham instead), fry the onions for 5 minutes over a moderate heat, until they are beginning to soften. Add the potatoes, and cook until crisp and golden. Add the meat: the meatballs, frankfurters, and Christmas ham or cooked pancetta. Stir frequently for a couple of minutes, then add the beetroot and warm through.

3. Finally, add the boiled eggs for the last minute of cooking (or, alternatively, add a fried egg to each plate). Serve with Swedish mustard and dill pickles.

Miso, soya and honey chipolatas

This is house-party food – great for putting in the middle of a table, or passing around with toothpicks and serviettes. In my (frequent) experience, they disappear almost faster than I can make a second batch, and that's saying something, considering how simple they are. I know I said that I would try to keep you out of the kitchen as much as possible, but truly these require little more than opening the door of the oven, and shoving a tray inside.

SERVES 10 OR MORE, IF YOU INSIST ON HAVING THAT MANY
PEOPLE AROUND (DO SCALE UP OR DOWN AS YOU SEE FIT)

60 chipolatas
2tbsp groundnut or vegetable oil
2tbsp brown miso paste

2tbsp soy sauce
2tbsp honey

1. Preheat the oven to 200°C/400°F/Gas 6. If the chipolatas are strung together, snip between them and toss them into a lined roasting pan, along with the oil (this is going to get messy and sticky, and the last thing you want is 3 a.m. washing up). Transfer to the oven and roast for 15 minutes.

2. Mix the miso, soy and honey together with a fork. Pull the chipolatas out of the oven, toss them around a bit, and then pour the sauce over the top. Toss again, making sure each sausage is covered. Return to the oven for a final 10 minutes before serving on a platter alongside some cocktail sticks/toothpicks.

Gin and thyme martini

When I was eighteen, I decided I needed to have a signature drink: something I always ordered when we went out. In my teen years, that drink was an amaretto on ice, something I have not tasted since I left Australia. The smell of it now (sweet, syrupy cyanide) sends me back to those years, to university and to parties with my old school friends. Over the next decade, I went through a series of 'signature drinks' – good Irish whiskey, an old fashioned, a whisky sour, a margarita. What I learnt is that I like far too many things to ever commit myself to one exclusive favourite. But also that, if absolutely forced to choose, more often than not it would be a martini.

MAKES ENOUGH FOR 1, BUT EASY TO SCALE ONCE YOU HAVE THE APPROPRIATE BOTTLES

INFUSED SIMPLE SYRUP
300g/10½oz sugar
150ml/⅔ cup water
1tbsp pink peppercorns
8 sprigs thyme, plus extra to serve

PER MARTINI
10ml/2tsp infused simple syrup
60ml/4tbsp gin (a citrus-heavy one)
5ml/1tsp dry vermouth
Ice

1. First, make the infused simple syrup. Bring the sugar, water, peppercorns and thyme to a simmer in a saucepan, and bubble gently for 10 minutes. Allow to cool, pour into a sterilized bottle and store in the fridge, where it will keep for a couple of weeks.

2. To assemble the drink, put a few cubes of ice and a little cold water in each cocktail glass, to chill them. Leave them for a few minutes, then tip the water and ice away, and gently wipe them out.

3. Put a handful of ice in cocktail shaker. Pour enough simple syrup for each person over the ice in the cocktail shaker, and stir, trying not to bash the ice. Pour in the gin and vermouth, stir again, and then immediately strain into your glass(es). Serve with a sprig of thyme.

Spiced beef

I know a roast joint of meat can seem like a scary prospect, but there really aren't many easier or more impressive dishes to put on the table. If you're nervous, a cheap meat thermometer will take away some of the fear, and reassure you that the beef is cooked properly inside. Honestly, all you really need to impress is the beef itself, but it's a spiced round of beef on the table at Aunt Kate's in Joyce's 'The Dead', alongside a fat goose and a great ham covered in breadcrumbs. In Ireland, this spiced beef would have been salted and rubbed in spice mix by your butcher months before the day itself, before being simmered in water, and eaten cold in thin slices. I'm keeping the traditional spice mix here, but cutting down on the curing time, instead encouraging you to give your joint of beef a night covered in spices in the fridge before it finds its way into the oven.

SERVES 6–8 (AND THERE WILL BE SOME LEFT OVER FOR A FEW SANDWICHES)

1tsp ground allspice
1tsp ground cloves
1tsp ground nutmeg
2tsp ground cinnamon

1tbsp black peppercorns, ground
2tbsp olive oil
2kg/4½lb topside beef

1. The day before you want to serve your beef, prepare the spice rub. Mix together the spices with the oil. Rub all over the topside, then cover, and leave in the fridge for 24 hours.

2. The next day, take the beef out of the fridge, and allow it to come to room temperature. Preheat your oven to 220°C/425°F/Gas 7. Place the beef into a tight-fitting roasting dish, and transfer to the oven. After 15 minutes, reduce the temperature to 170°C/325°F/Gas 3.

3. Cook the meat at the lower temperature for a further 9 minutes per 450g/1lb for rare or 11 minutes per 450g/1lb for medium rare – so a 2kg/4½lb joint you're roasting rare should take 40 minutes (55 minutes in total, including the higher temperature start). If you're using a meat thermometer, for rare it should read 48°C/118°F when poked into the centre of the joint, or 55°C/131°F for medium rare.

4. Take the beef out of the oven, and rest it under foil for at least 30 minutes before slicing into it. Serve with radicchio salad (p160), and some buttery mashed potato, or the cheesy orzo on p165.

Radicchio salad

This salad is a thing of beauty. It works well alongside the spiced beef (p158), as well as the cheesy orzo (p165) – the richness of both cries out for something sharp and bitter, which this delivers in spades. Toss it together just before you bring it to the table; the radicchio leaves should be fresh and crisp. If you make this salad during January (it's great then too), keep an eye out for blood oranges; it's even more stunning with them in place of regular oranges.

SERVES 8

1 large head of radicchio
2 oranges
1tsp balsamic vinegar
1tbsp olive oil

Sea salt and black pepper
Fronds from 10 small sprigs of dill
3tbsp pine nuts, toasted in a pan until golden

1. Take the radicchio apart and give the leaves a rinse under cold water. Pat dry and set aside.

2. To prepare the oranges, slice the top and bottoms off, and then slice off the peel in strips, following the curve of the orange, ensuring you remove as much of the pith as you can with each slice. Trim any pith left behind. Slice the oranges into thin slices, right through the core, and then remove the seeds. Set the orange slices aside, and sweep any juice on your chopping board into a bowl.

3. Put the balsamic vinegar into the bowl with the orange juice, and whisk in the olive oil. Season with salt and pepper.

4. Toss the radicchio in the dressing and arrange on a serving plate, then lay the orange slices on top. Add the dill fronds and sprinkle the pine nuts over the top. Serve immediately.

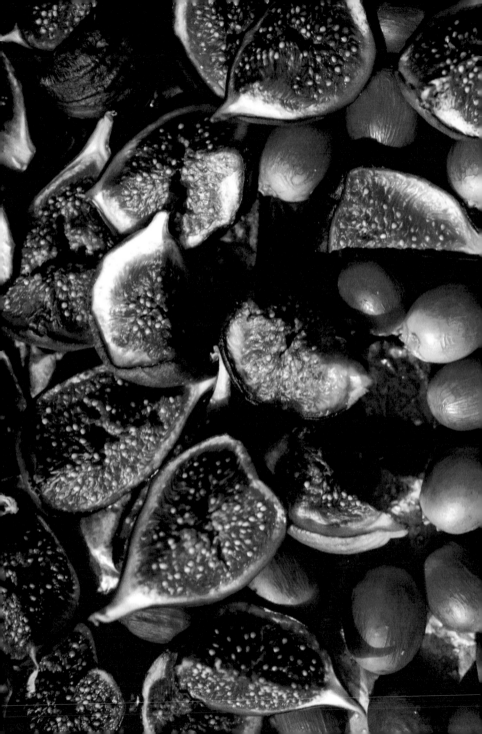

What would happen if I ate caviar, turtle soup, turkey, plum pudding, mince pies, biscuit tortoni, hot rolls with butter and crystallised fruit and drank hock, Champagne, Port and liqueurs. Would I die?

'Another Christmas Carol', P. G. Wodehouse

Those days that run from Christmas and New Year are some of my favourite of the year. After the hustle and bustle of the Christmas season, they encourage a laziness and lethargy, as we all struggle to make it out of pyjamas, or much further than a relaxed amble around the village. I read more in this week than in any other week of the year, and tackle puzzles in a single day that would otherwise take weeks of gradual effort. It's a time for quiet, and books, and easy film watching. Getting back to work before January seems futile – there are just so few days left. The one year I returned to the office straight after Boxing Day was one of the most productive periods I have ever had – no one emailed me, or stopped me in the hallway for an unnecessary conversation. A round of teas for the office was just me making one for myself. But I never volunteered to do it again – I crave those days of doing blissfully little.

Being able to do blissfully little is aided by the reality that the week after Christmas is a week of leftovers. A week of finding lids to fit Tupperware (and never being able to lay your hands on the one that will fit the box that you have *just* poured gravy into), playing a sort of strange fridge Tetris with mismatched boxes and bags and questionable things wrapped in foil. If I make it sound like a trial, I don't mean to. After time spent in the kitchen over Christmas it is reassuring to be faced with leftovers that need little more than to be gently warmed through – or can be turned into something new if you can muster up the energy.

One early Cotswolds Christmas, we all stayed put well into the early days of January. It was a long time to all be under one roof, when the weather is appalling and there is no work to be done, but it is a week (and a bit) that I remember fondly. With a fridge and pantry filled with as-yet unconsumed riches, we paired off and allocated ourselves evenings to cook. What followed was a *Come Dine With Me* sort of battle-of-the-dinners. We were each handed some leftover ingredients: half a bag of parsnips, a panettone, an opened bottle of red wine, the rest of the ham, and were left to rustle up dinner. We themed our menus: a round-the-world trip, a tribute to the Christopher Guest film *A Mighty Wind*, worked on table decorations, and spent the afternoon shooing the competition from the kitchen.

What ended up on the table was an occasionally ridiculous collection of dishes – meals that rarely 'went together' but that we consumed with gusto regardless. And those mad menus we created are still stuck to the fridge, a decade later. For the rest of our meals, we ate the leftovers more simply, with a splodge of mustard or some lingonberry jam on the side, or with an egg on the top – as ever, a fried egg turns the most repetitive of leftovers (roasted sprouts, Christmas ham, Jansson's temptation) into a meal. After the pressure to get everything right on Christmas Day – the potatoes perfectly crisp, the meat tender, the sprouts just on the edge of undercooked – being irreverent with the leftovers in the days leading up to New Year is a joy. Like my propensity to stay in pyjamas and re-read old favourites – murder mysteries and children's classics and Jilly Cooper – the key is not to expect too much of ourselves. Ease and comfort and familiarity above all else.

Cheesy orzo

If you had a cheeseboard at any point over Christmas, it's almost inevitable that you'll have some odd ends of cheese languishing in the fridge. Though I've detailed a basic recipe below, feel free to play around with adding whatever you have to hand – most hard cheeses will work well, as will the last of a tub of ricotta, a soft cheese torn into pieces, or the final bit of a wedge of blue, crumbled in. Serve this with something sharp and crisp – the radicchio salad (p160) or the pickled sprouts (p18) are perfect.

SERVES 8

1tbsp butter
500g/1lb 2oz dried orzo
125g/scant 1½ cups grated Cheddar
40g/½ cup grated Parmesan
250g/9oz soft mozzarella, chopped into 1cm/½in square chunks

Leaves from 10 sprigs of thyme
850ml/generous 3½ cups chicken stock
2 cloves garlic, minced
1tbsp balsamic vinegar

1. Preheat your oven to 200°C/400°F/Gas 6. Grease a baking dish with the butter, then tip in the dried orzo. Add the cheeses, thyme leaves, chicken stock and garlic. Cover with foil and transfer to the oven for 25 minutes.

2. Remove the foil, pour over the vinegar, and give the pasta a stir. Return the dish, uncovered, to the oven for a final 10 minutes, then allow to cool for 5 minutes before serving.

Pear, chocolate and sherry cake

If you're planning on bringing a dessert to the table on New Year's Eve, make it a cake. Something that can be prepared in advance, sitting on the side as you eat and make merry, ready and waiting for your guests. This cake, a damp, rich joy of a dessert, is exactly what I want late on a cold winter's night. A spoonful of crème fraîche, or a scoop of ice cream, would prove welcome alongside it.

SERVES 8

FRUIT
3 almost-ripe pears
1tbsp butter
2tbsp light brown sugar
3tbsp sherry

BATTER
200g/¾ cup + 2tbsp butter

200g/1 cup light brown sugar
3 eggs
125g/1¼ cups ground almonds
25g/3tbsp plain/all-purpose flour
50g/½ cup cocoa powder
1½tsp baking powder
A pinch of salt

1. Peel the pears, slice in half and scoop out the core. Melt the butter, sugar and sherry in a frying pan over a low heat, then lay the pear halves in the pan, cooking them on both sides until softened a little.

2. Preheat the oven to 160°C/320°F/Gas 2–3. For the batter, cream the butter and sugar together until light and smooth, then beat in the eggs. Fold in the ground almonds, flour, cocoa powder, baking powder and salt. Finally, fold in the liquid the pears were cooked in.

3. Grease and line an 18cm/7in loose-bottomed cake pan. Put the pears cut side down on the bottom of the pan, and then spoon the cake batter over the top and level it off. Bake for 40 minutes until a knife inserted in the centre comes out clean. Cool for half an hour in the pan, and then entirely on a wire rack, or invert immediately, so the pears are on top, and eat warm, in crumbly slices, if you prefer.

Panettone bread and butter pudding

I've never reached the end of the Christmas season without at least a bit of panettone left. It's great used as French toast – cut into slices, dipped into beaten eggs and milk and fried in butter – but is really never better than it is here. I've been making this for years and am so wedded to it that I'll keep my eyes peeled for supermarket offers on the good panettone in the days following Christmas.

SERVES 8

600g/1lb 5oz panettone
100g/7tbsp butter, softened
3tbsp whisky or brandy
2tbsp golden caster/superfine sugar

250ml/1 cup whole milk
250ml/1 cup double/heavy cream
5 eggs
1tsp vanilla bean paste

1. Cut the panettone into generous slices, and lay out on your work surface for a couple of hours if you have time. Once you come to baking, you're going to need two baking dishes that fit inside each other, as you need to create a bain-marie. Dedicate some time to looking for ones you can use while your panettone is going a little stale.

2. Preheat the oven to 150°C/300°F/Gas 2. Blend the butter, whisky or brandy, and sugar together with a fork, and spread generously onto the slices of panettone. Arrange in the smaller baking dish – the pieces mostly standing up so that their crusts poke up over the top a little. Whisk together the milk, cream, eggs and vanilla paste. Pour over the panettone, and leave to sit for half an hour.

3. Place the filled dish inside the larger empty dish, place both in the oven and, before you close the door, fill the bottom dish with just boiled water, so that it comes at least halfway up the side of the top dish. Bake for 50 minutes, until the custard is puffed and barely set.

Toast, Vegemite and dippy eggs

When I started to go to parties, Mum offered a bit of invaluable hangover-avoiding-related advice: always have a slice of toast with Vegemite and a glass of water before bed. Though I'm still, nearly two decades later, religious about the late-night slice of toast, my favourite time to eat it is actually the next morning, when the eggs I'm far too lazy to boil at 2 a.m. come into play. Reading Amor Towles' *Rules of Civility*, where the money set aside for post-drinking toast and eggs is spent on cocktails by 9.30 p.m. on New Year's Eve, fills me with visceral fear. Always set a little money aside for toast and eggs (and Vegemite).

ENOUGH FOR 1 (THOUGH YOU MAY NEED TO GO BACK FOR MORE)

2 eggs at room temperature
1 slice of sourdough bread (or whatever you have around)

A generous amount of butter
A silly amount of Vegemite (or Marmite, I guess, if you're a heathen)

1. Put a small pan of water on to boil, and make a pot of coffee, so it's ready for you when you need it. Once the pan of water is bubbling furiously, turn down to a steady simmer and lower the eggs in on a spoon (so they don't hit the bottom of the pan and crack). Set a timer for 3½ minutes.

2. While the eggs are bustling about in the pan, do a little bustling about yourself. Toast the bread to your liking, spread thickly with butter, then as thickly as you can stand with Vegemite, and cut into soldiers.

3. When your timer goes off, run cold water over the eggs, then put into eggcups, and slice the tops off. You'll need a small spoon to scoop the last of the egg out of the shell, but try and get as much out as you can using the toast as your implement.

Una's turkey curry buffet

I wasn't sold on turkey until I made it one Thanksgiving, with my American friend Fiona and a few pals. Honestly, for taste, I'd prefer a chicken (or two). But Fiona and I, both a bit 'meh' on the big bird, orchestrated a plan to confit the legs and wings and to roast the breast separately. It worked a treat – each part sang. Inevitably, with only six of us at the table, we had leftovers. This is my favourite way to employ them: Una's turkey curry from *Bridget Jones's Diary*, made good (she puts bananas in hers – please, please don't).

SERVES 4 – OR MORE IF YOU SCALE UP, DEPENDING ON HOW
PLENTIFUL YOUR LEFTOVERS ARE

2tbsp fat (either leftover from the bird, or vegetable oil or clarified butter)
1 large brown onion, thinly sliced
2 cloves garlic, finely chopped
2tsp ground cumin
2tsp ground coriander
1tsp ground ginger
1tsp ground turmeric
4 cardamom pods, lightly crushed
2 large potatoes, roughly chopped (use leftover roast potatoes if you like)

2 large carrots, roughly chopped (again, leftover roasted ones are fine)
400ml/1¾ cups turkey stock* or chicken stock
300g/10½oz leftover turkey, stripped from the carcass and shredded
200g/7oz frozen peas
3tbsp natural/plain yogurt
A large handful of chopped coriander/cilantro

* You can make the stock with the turkey carcass, once you have stripped it. Roughly chop 2 celery sticks, 2 carrots and 2 brown onions and add them to a saucepan with 10 peppercorns and the turkey carcass. Cover with water and bring to a simmer over a medium heat. After 1 hour, strain and reserve the stock.

1. Warm the fat in a large saucepan over a medium heat. Add the onion and stir for 5 minutes until softened and translucent, but not browned. Add the garlic and cook for another couple of minutes, until fragrant. Add the spices and cook, stirring frequently, for at least 5 minutes. By this stage, the onion should be completely coated with

the spices and the saucepan should be wonderfully fragrant.

2. Add the potatoes and carrots. If they are raw, stir them for 5 minutes or so, to soften them. If they are leftover roast veggies, just give them a minute.

3. Add the stock and stir well. Bring to the boil and simmer away for 10 minutes or so, until the vegetables are tender and the sauce slightly reduced. Add the shredded meat, the peas, and finally stir the yogurt through.

4. Cook for another couple of minutes to ensure the turkey is hot, then remove from the heat and stir the coriander leaves through. Serve with rice, mango chutney and poppadoms. And a beer.

These are my New Year's resolutions:
1. I will be true to Pandora.
2. I will bring my bike in at night.
3. I will not read unworthy books.

The Secret Diary of Adrian Mole Aged 13¾, Sue Townsend

I am an enthusiastic devotee to the concept of a new start. Freshly sharpened pencils; a blank notebook waiting for words in some sort of thoughtful order; a clean fridge, stripped down to its barest minimum and crying out for ingredients. But it's an aspiration I associate more with September – that post-summer, back-to-school boost of energy, or March, when I thrust open the windows and the house smells of fresh linen and daffodils. The beginning of the year, on the other hand, seems somehow less like a new beginning. The decorations are still up, and most of my friends and family have managed to avoid a proper, committed returning to work. And so New Year's Day, whether alcohol-related or not, is a hangover.

It is, therefore, an odd time to commit oneself to difficult-to-keep promises – to gym memberships or running plans, to abstinence of any form. January is cold and grey and dark enough as it is. But my two early literary guides in diary writing were Bridget and Adrian, and I (ill-advisedly) followed their lead when it came to picking New Year's resolutions each year. Unsurprising, then, that I have long viewed resolutions as something I'm bound to fail at. Bridget Jones's pages-long annual vows to 'be positive about everyone', not to smoke or to date dreadful men, and to stop buying books by 'unreadable literary authors to put impressively on shelves' never last into February. Oddly, it's Adrian Mole's extensive list of slightly more achievable, and very specific, resolutions that has become inspirational in adulthood:

clean the bath after each use, do daily back-stretching exercises, study hard, and forgive Barry Kent his multiple sins. It's a decent plan for the year.

A couple of years ago, at a New Year's party, my friend Misha encouraged us all to write down a dozen hopes and plans for the coming year. It gave us an opportunity to think about what we really wanted. For me: to find a good therapist, to read more translated fiction, to book a trip to Tokyo, to try more British cheeses, to settle on a place to call home. We made lists filled with a mix of hopeful and achievable goals and it felt like a good note to be entering the New Year on – so I now commend it to you. Leave new fitness regimes for the longer, sunnier days of March, and enter the year filled with hope instead. Or, take a leaf out of Virginia Woolf's book (her diary, actually) – her resolutions for 1931 are some of the best I've seen.

Here are my resolutions for the next 3 months;
the next lap of the year.
First, to have none. Not to be tied.
Second, to be free & kindly with myself, not
goading it to parties: to sit rather privately
reading in the studio.
To make a good job of The Waves.
To care nothing for making money.
As for Nelly, to stop irritation by the assurance
that nothing is worth irritation: if it comes
back, she must go. Then not to slip this time
into the easiness of letting her stay.
Then—well the chief resolution is the
most important—not to make resolutions.
Sometimes to read, sometimes not to read.
To go out yes—but stay at home in spite of
being asked.
As for clothes, I think to buy good ones.

Virginia Woolf, personal diary, January 2, 1931

RECIPE INDEX

A

almonds
  Almond and pistachio biscotti 29
  Christmas cake 139–41
  Christmas pudding 135–6
  Pear, chocolate and sherry cake 166
apples
  Apple, pear and chilli chutney 17
  Beetroot salad 99
  Christmas dinner 117–8
  Christmas pudding 135–6
  Latkes with apple sauce or spiced
    mayonnaise 50–1
  Mince pies 67–9
apricots, Christmas cake 139–41

B

bacon, Stuffing 121
beef
  Spiced beef 158–9
  Swedish meatballs 89–90
beetroot
  Beetroot gravadlax with cucumber pickle
    and horseradish sauce 87–8
  Beetroot salad 99
  Pytt i panna 154
berries, mixed, Meringues and cream 103–4
brandy
  French bonbons 35–7
  Lussekatter (saffron buns) 83–4
  One for Paul F. 48
  Panettone bread and butter pudding 167
bread
  Christmas pudding 135–6
  Crab cakes 56–7
  Ginger beer ham on brioche buns 52–4
  Grief wellington 124–5
  Jansson's temptation 96–7
  Not-sausage rolls 64–5
  Panettone bread and butter pudding 167
  Porcini mushroom arancini 59–60
  Stuffing 121
  Swedish meatballs 89–90

  Toast, Vegemite and dippy eggs 168
Brussels sprouts
  Crispy Brussels sprouts 127
  Pickled sprouts 18
Buckwheat blinis for breakfast 115–6

C

cabbage, Grief wellington 124–5
Campari, Liqueur cocktails 49
capers, Crab cakes 56–7
carrots
  Christmas pudding 135–6
  Grief wellington 124–5
  Start-in-advance gravy 118–20
  Una's turkey curry buffet 171–2
caviar
  Gubbröra 85
  Jansson's temptation 96–7
cavolo nero, Greens for sustenance 66
celeriac, Grief wellington 124–5
celery, Start-in-advance gravy 118–20
Champagne cocktails 48–9
cheese
  Cheesy orzo 165
  Endive and walnut salad 98
  Grief wellington 124–5
  Porcini mushroom arancini 59–60
  Potted Stilton and rosemary and rye
    crackers 14–5
cherries
  Cherry and pecan brownies 70–1
  Christmas cake 139–41
  Sparkling sherry 49
chicken, Start-in-advance gravy 118–20
chilli sauce, Greens for sustenance 66
chipolatas
  Miso, soya and honey chipolatas 155
  Stuffing 121
chocolate
  Cherry and pecan brownies 70–1
  French bonbons 35–7
Christmas cake 139–41
Christmas dinner 117–8

P

Panettone bread and butter pudding 167
parsnips, Grief wellington 124–5
pasta, Cheesy orzo 165
pears
    Apple, pear and chilli chutney 17
    Endive and walnut salad 98
    Pear, chocolate and sherry cake 166
peas, Una's turkey curry buffet 171–2
pecans, Cherry and pecan brownies 70–1
Pepparkakor 100
peppercorns
    Gin and thyme martini 156
    Pickled sprouts 18
    Potted Stilton and rosemary and rye
        crackers 14–5
Pickled sprouts 18
pine nuts, Radicchio salad 160
pistachios, Almond and pistachio biscotti 29
pomegranate seeds, Endive and walnut
    salad 98
Porcini mushroom arancini 59–60
pork
    Ginger beer ham on brioche buns 52–4
    Pytt i panna 154
    Stuffing 121
    Swedish meatballs 89–90
Port
    Potted Stilton and rosemary and rye
        crackers 14–5
    Smoking bishop 142–3
Port wine, Mince pies 67–9
potatoes
    Crab cakes 56–7
    Jansson's temptation 96–7
    Latkes with apple sauce or spiced
        mayonnaise 50–1
    Pytt i panna 154
    Una's turkey curry buffet 171–2
Potted Stilton and rosemary and rye
    crackers 14–5
prunes
    Christmas cake 139–41
    French bonbons 35–7

puff pastry
    Grief wellington 124–5
    Not-sausage rolls 64–5
Pytt i panna 154

Q

quinces, Spiced quince jelly 26–7

R

Radicchio salad 160
raisins
    Christmas cake 139–41
    Lussekatter (saffron buns) 83–4
    Mince pies 67–9
raspberries, Meringues and cream
    103–4
redcurrants, Meringues and cream
    103–4
rice
    Porcini mushroom arancini 59–60
    Stovetop rice pudding 82
Roasted figs for a cheeseboard 131–2
Rosemary and chilli roasted nuts 19
rosewater, Turkish delight 32–4
rum, Christmas pudding 135–6

S

salmon
    Beetroot gravadlax with cucumber pickle
        and horseradish sauce 87–8
    Buckwheat blinis for breakfast 115–6
sesame seeds
    Crispy Brussels sprouts 127
    Ginger beer ham on brioche buns 52–4
    Greens for sustenance 66
    Not-sausage rolls 64–5
sherry
    Pear, chocolate and sherry cake 166
    Potted Stilton and rosemary and rye
        crackers 14–5
    Sparkling sherry 49
sloe royale 49
Smoking bishop 142–3

READING AND WATCHING INDEX

THANKS

This book consumed my life last winter: midnight recipe testing, early mornings planning and reading, endless writing playlists filled with carols, long days with the camera trying to steal as much light as we could. And then, just as it was sent away for editing, and spring began to arrive, we were plunged into lockdown. I am writing this final page in late spring, desperately missing the people and houses and dining tables that inhabit the stories throughout these pages. My hope is that, by the time you all have this book in your hands, we're able to properly celebrate Christmas together.

In the meantime, I have people to thank.

Immense thanks to Maddy, for calling me last year about a 'small, by the till pamphlet' that quickly became this beautiful little book. It is, as ever, a true joy to work with you.

Enormous thanks to Zoe, for being a reassuring and supportive voice, and for your endless championing.

Colossal thanks to Lean, who didn't blink an eye when our laidback December time together turned into a proper, full-on photo shoot. We had barely enough time to breathe and take in the beauty of the tree but, Lean, I think these shots are some of my favourite we've ever done.

Massive thanks to Jessie who returned from maternity leave to put this book together, and made each page sing. I have loved being able to work even more closely than normal with you on this one (despite the necessary social distancing).

Considerable thanks to the team at Head of Zeus who have produced this book with such love and care, under incredibly odd and unprecedented circumstances.

Immeasurable thanks to Ella, who read this entire book cover to cover while holding a phone to her ear during lockdown, who reassured me, whipped me into shape, and told me exactly what the book needed, and what I needed to hear. Thank you, always, for the prison yard, and for being my lockdown colleague and dear, dear friend.

Affectionate thanks, as ever, to my work wife Liv, who was a sounding board for so many of these recipes, and who helped me work through a million little niggles while we catered Christmas parties and Crisis Christmas shifts. Time in the kitchen with you is my favourite of all possible times. And, of course, thanks to Sam and Ruby, for sharing your home with me so often.

Heartfelt thanks to those writers I love and admire, who have been so generous in their support of my books, especially Bee Wilson, Nina Stibbe, Olia Hercules, Ruby Tandoh, Sarah Perry, and Tessa Kiros. And, most especially, to Diana Henry, for all your kindness and bolstering.

Fond thanks to my friends and neighbours, whose hands (and faces!) are throughout this book: Berta, Dolly, Mackie, Misha, Nina, Rosa, Tilly, and Tom.

Inordinate thanks to my extended family, and all the families I have spent Christmas in the company of. This book is built on memories of egg salad and leftovers with the Hermans, Will's family trifle, and the Duncans' air conditioning. I tried naming you all in person, but it ran to some three pages. I hope you will forgive my simply thanking you all in person next time I see you.

Finally, and most of all, loving thanks to Anna, Cheryl, Chris, Dad, Geoff, Justin, Luce, Mia, Mum, and Tom, for so many Christmases spent in your glorious and impossibly brilliant company. Thanks for the recipes and rituals and everything contained within these pages. And to Ingela, of course, for sharing so much of your Christmas with me. I shall endeavor, always, to do these small bits of it justice.

EXTENDED COPYRIGHT

Extract from *4.50 from Paddington* by Agatha Christie. Copyright © Agatha Christie, 1957. Reprinted by permission of HarperCollins Publishers Ltd.

Extract from *Ordinary People* by Diana Evans. Copyright © Diana Evans, 2018. Reproduced from 2018 hardback edition, Chatto and Windus, an imprint of Vintage, part of the Penguin Random House Group.

Extract from *Bridget Jones's Diary* by Helen Fielding. Copyright © Helen Fielding, 1996. Used by permission of Viking Books, an imprint of Penguin Publishing Group, a division of Penguin Random House LLC (USA). Used by permission of Picador (UK). All rights reserved.

Extract from *The Story of Holly and Ivy* by Rumer Godden. Copyright © Rumer Godden, 1953. Rights holder Curtis Brown (UK). Reproduced from 2016 ebook edition, Macmillan Children's Books.

Extract from *The Box of Delights* by John Masefield. Reprinted by permission of The Society of Authors as the Literary Representatives of the Estate of John Masefield.

Extract from *Christmas Pudding* by Nancy Mitford. Published by Penguin, 1932. Copyright © The Estate of Nancy Mitford. Reproduced by permission of the Estate c/o Rogers, Coleridge & White Ltd., 20 Powis Mews, London W11 1JN and Penguin Books.

Extract from *Findus at Christmas* by Sven Nordqvist. Reprinted by permission of Hawthorn Press.

Extract from *A Vicarage Family* by Noel Streatfeild (Copyright © Noel Streatfeild) Reprinted by permission of A.M. Heath & Co Ltd.

Extract from *The Secret Diary of Adrian Mole, Aged 13 and ¾* by Sue Townsend. Copyright © Sue Townsend, 1982. Reproduced from 2002 paperback edition, Puffin Books, an imprint of The Random House Group Ltd.

Extract from 'Another Christmas Carol' from *The World of Mr Mulliner* by P.G. Wodehouse. Copyright © The Estate of P.G. Wodehouse. Reproduced by permission of the Estate c/o Rogers, Coleridge & White Ltd., 20 Powis Mews, London W11 1JN.

Every effort has been made to contact copyright holders. The publisher would be grateful to rectify any omissions or errors in future reprints or editions of this book.